HOW HERETICS DISMANTLED THE MEDIEVAL CATHOLIC PATRIARCHAL FAMILY UNIT TO USHER IN MODERN SECULARISM

Insights from the Reformation and French Revolution on the Shift from Christendom to Secularism

By

Christopher E. Ross B.S., MBA, M.S.

© 2024 Sanctus Virtue Publishing, Dearborn, Michigan

All rights reserved

ISBN: 979-8-9916647-4-5

Library of Congress catalogue and card number: 2024924096

Printed in the United States of America

Contents

Introduction 1

Chapter 1:

The Fundamental Role of Family in Society and the State 7

Patriarchy's Influence on State Authority in Traditional Christendom 13

The Family as a Business Unit in Traditional Christendom 15

The Foundational Role of Family in Civilization: Nurturing Love, Productivity, and Stability 16

The Vital Role of Procreation in Sustaining Civilization ... 17

Chapter 2:

The Sacred Covenant of Marriage: Fidelity, Offspring, and Sacrament 19

What Constituted Marriage 20

The Significance of Marriage and Property in Traditional Christendom 21

Marriage, Divorce, and Property: A Historical Perspective 23

The Significance of Consent in Traditional Western Marriages 25

The Moral and Social Implications of Contraception in Christendom 27

The Church's Role in Marriage and Family Jurisdiction .. 28

Family-Based Law Enforcement and Blood Feuds in
Traditional Christendom 30

Gender Roles in Traditional Christendom 31

Chapter 3:

The Evolution of Divorce and Marriage Laws in
Traditional Christendom 35

The Role of Children in Traditional Christendom:
Legitimacy, Education, and Heirship 38

The Transformation of Adultery/Fornication Laws and
Morality in Traditional Christendom 40

Homosexuality 45

The Staunch Opposition to Polygamy in Traditional
Christendom 46

Chapter 4:

Marriage, Family, and Power: The Lasting Impact of the
Reformation and the French Revolution 48

Why Traditional Christendom Favored Celibacy as
Opposed the Marriage? 50

The Evolution of Divorce Practices in the Wake of the
Reformation 51

Luther's Challenge to Chastity and Celibacy in the
Catholic Church 53

Luther's Challenge to the Sacrament of Marriage and its
Impact on Family Law and Authority 54

Challenging Traditional Hierarchies and Gender Roles
in the Wake of the Reformation 59

The Catholic Sacramental Model of Marriage and Its
Threefold Purpose 61

The Influence and Regulations of Catholic Canon Law on Marriage and Family 63

Marriage in the Enlightenment Era 65

How the French Revolution Shaped Family and Marriage in the West 67

St. John Chrysostom on Christian Marriage: Biblical Foundations, Bishop's Role, and Catholic Teachings on Family Life 76

Concluding Teachings on the Catechism of the Catholic Church and the Canon Law Regarding Marriage and Family 77

Further Insights into St. John Chrysostom's Teachings on the Bishop's Role in Christian Marriage 78

The Sacred Bond of Marriage and Mutual Submission 80

Further Insights into Marriage in the Light of Canon Law and the Catechism of the Catholic Church 82

Conclusion 84

Bibliography 88

Explore More from Sanctus Virtue Publishing 89

Introduction

Family, often regarded as the most crucial institution on Earth, plays an indispensable role in shaping the social fabric and governing the political structures of any given state. Scholars and philosophers, both in antiquity and in modern times, consider the family as the micro-unit of a state, with the state itself serving as the macro-unit. Family's centrality to human civilization lies in its capacity to impart essential skills for survival, social interaction, and the formation of individual identities.

As Aristotle underscored, family and marriage constitute the bedrock of the polis, for each city-state comprises households, and these households rely on interdependent unions. Family, the crucible of human existence, provides the primary framework for fulfilling biological, psychological, and spiritual needs. It serves as the cornerstone of socialization and functions as a mini-autonomous government, an educational institution, a spiritual and religious educator, a mini-justice system, and a fundamental contributor to producing goods and services.

Moreover, the family is the conduit through which property passes from generation to generation. As such, marriage and family represent the core means by which the legacy of religion, culture, heritage, and property is perpetuated. In the family context, love and support among spouses and children are nurtured, ensuring the continuity of family names, traditions, and societal stability. Proper marriage and family structures are ideal for raising children with appropriate nurture and education, forging natural bonds of kinship, and nurturing mutual support among family members.

The historical tapestry of Western Christendom reveals a profound interplay between the monarchical structures of the state and the domestic hierarchy of the family. In this traditional Christian framework, the state, often called the "commonwealth," and the family, dubbed the "domestic commonwealth," rested on the pillars of absolute authority. Just as the king or emperor wielded supreme authority over the state, the male head of the household, the paterfamilias, exercised absolute rule within the family unit. This dual structure resonated with the deeply ingrained notion of male authority dating back to the origins of human civilization.

The father's dominion over the family mirrored the king's dominion over the multitude of families in the state. In this context, the transition from familial obedience to royal authority occurred seamlessly, as people were already accustomed to deferring to the male head of their households. The hierarchical framework of the family, where the eldest male held sway, found its parallel in the state's authority, with the king at its helm. The family unit served as the microcosm of the state, and as individuals obeyed their fathers, they readily extended that obedience to the king, fostering political cohesion and allegiance.

The historical concept of consent in traditional Western marriages bears witness to the intricate interplay between Church, state, and family in the evolution of marital customs. In the Western tradition, a father's consent was paramount when it came to a daughter's choice of marriage. A person daring to marry against parental consent risked excommunication by the Church and legal invalidation of the union, even if the bride herself consented. Such a union, characterized as abduction, often incurred severe penalties, including exile and, in some cases, even death. As the power of the Church grew within traditional Christendom, the emphasis on consent gained further complexity.

For a marriage to be considered legitimate, consent was required from not just the bride and groom but also from the Church, state, and parents. The gravity of this tripartite consent was rooted in the multifaceted implications of marriage. It transcended mere romantic love and embraced property rights, inheritance, titles, lands, and societal responsibilities. By ensuring the alignment of these three key parties— Church, state, and family—marriage served as a cornerstone for societal stability and safeguarding property, inheritance, and social order. It was not merely a romantic union but a binding contract with profound moral and social consequences.

In the tapestry of traditional Christendom, children held a cherished position, not only as a means of perpetuating the family lineage but also as carriers of the family's values and heritage. This era, quite distinct from contemporary times, did not consign its young to government-run public schools. Instead, children were entrusted to qualified tutors, and discipline was met with sternness, reflecting the deeply held belief that a father's love was demonstrated through his involvement in his child's education. To provide a secure future for their offspring, fathers sought to amass wealth, securing their children's inheritance. A son's prosperous life and ability to care for his father in old age became a testament to the love and dedication of a father in traditional Christendom.

Noble lineages further honed their children's skills, sending sons to train as knights and daughters to refine their social graces. Every effort was dedicated to ensuring that children would have the means to lead fulfilling lives. The father's role as a guide, protector, and provider was paramount. A journey into the past reveals the stark differences between legitimate and illegitimate children, where legitimacy conferred rights and obligations on the family. Legitimate children were under the watchful eye of the paterfamilias, a position of near-absolute authority. As we delve deeper into this historical analysis, we explore the transformation of adultery and fornication laws, the staunch opposition to polygamy, and the significance of celibacy. The impact of the Reformation on family, Church, and state presents a compelling narrative of shifting powers and authorities, a transformation that continues to shape society today.

The role of children in traditional Christendom was deeply ingrained with a complex interplay of legitimacy, education, and heirship. In this society, children were not merely the offspring of their parents; they represented the continuation of a family's lineage, property, and values. Traditional Christendom placed significant emphasis on the duties and responsibilities of parents, especially fathers, in ensuring the well-being and success of their children. This extended from securing a legitimate status for their offspring to meticulous oversight of their education, shaping them into morally upstanding adults who could perpetuate the family legacy. Moreover, the concept of legitimacy had far-reaching implications, distinguishing between rightful heirs and those born outside the bounds of wedlock, thus creating a clear division in the inheritance and social privileges allocated to children. The nurturing and upbringing of children were not merely acts of love but integral elements of preserving the family's heritage and faith.

This treatise delves into the intricate dynamics of the family within the historical tapestry of Western Christendom, revealing its multifaceted role as the cornerstone of society, a parallel structure to the state's monarchical authority, and a pivotal player in the evolution of marriage customs and the interplay of consent. As we explore the cherished position of children and the profound implications of legitimacy, education, and heirship, it becomes evident that the family's significance extends beyond love and support, encompassing the transmission of values, heritage, and societal stability. This chapter offers an in-depth analysis of how the family, Church, and state interweaved to shape a unique socio-political landscape in traditional Christendom and how it changed during the Reformation, Enlightenment, and French Revolution, with lasting implications for contemporary society.

Chapter 1:

THE FUNDAMENTAL ROLE OF FAMILY IN SOCIETY AND THE STATE

Family is most likely the most important institution on Earth. The way the family is governed during any time in history has almost everything to do with the political structure of any given state because the family is considered by many scholars and philosophers in antiquity and today as the micro-unit of a state, while the state itself acting as the macro-unit. Family is vital to human civilization because it is the very means by which human beings learn the vital skills of human survival and social interaction.

It is the very place where people get their sense of identity.[1] For example, Aristotle (384-321 BC) taught that marriage and family are the foundation of the polis (city-state) itself because every city-state is composed of households and that these very households are composed of unions that are co-dependent upon one another, as in it takes both a male and female union to produce a child.[2] Family is the primary mechanism by which a person gets his or her primary biological,

---

[1] Gies, Frances. Marriage and the Family in the Middle Ages (Medieval Life) (p. 3). HarperCollins. Kindle Edition.
[2] Witte, J. (2012). *From sacrament to contract: marriage, religion, and law in the Western tradition*. Louisville (Kentucky); Westminster John Knox Press. pg. 19

psychological, and spiritual needs met; it is where the primary means of socialization occurs.[3]

Looking at family from a historical perspective, it was the very unit that acted as a type of mini-autonomous government within a state because it acted as a type of political unit, a place where education was taught, where spiritual and religious teachings were taught, a mini-justice system, and one of the primary units of products of goods and services.[4] Family is also the primary means of how property is transmitted from one generation to the next.[5] According to Witte (2012), "...Voltaire's quip, "Among Christians, the family is either a little Church, a little state, or a little club" blessed by nature and nature's God."[6]

Marriage and family are the primary means to foster mutual support and love between spouses and children, the mechanism for children to carry on the family name, religion, culture, heritage, and family property.[7] The very continuance of family is so important that entire states depend upon the continuance of family because each generation would serve as heirs to the family property, uphold the household name, religion, etc., which are the very building blocks of the continuation of a state.[8]

Proper marriage and family are the proper means for bringing children into the world, with the proper

---

[3] Gies, Frances. Marriage and the Family in the Middle Ages (Medieval Life) (pp. 6-7). HarperCollins. Kindle Edition.
[4] Ibid.
[5] Ibid.
[6] Witte, J. (2012). *From sacrament to contract: marriage, religion, and law in the Western tradition.* Louisville (Kentucky); Westminster John Knox Press. pg. 2
[7] Ibid.
[8] Ibid, pg. 25.

nurture and education until adulthood, providing the means of natural bonds of kinship that lead to the proper service and support of each other, especially in times of need, young age, old age, in sickness and in health.[9] Christendom only allowed for heterosexual unions and outlawed that which contradicted heterosexual marriages meant to produce children and societal stability, such as incest, homosexuality (sodomy), pederasty, bestiality, contraception, etc.[10] Marriage is needed because the human female species requires assistance raising children. It is nearly impossible for a female on her own to raise children by herself without assistance; therefore, God and nature have intended male and female unions for the proper care of each other and children.

It is against God and nature for a man to produce a child with a woman and leave her to have relations with another woman; it is the practice of fornicators to do such an action, and it was forbidden in Christendom.[11] God and nature have placed it within the male and female to stay together for the sake of dependent children, and marriage is the best avenue for children to be raised. Traditional Christendom puts strong importance on fidelity in marriage because if a man knows for certain that a woman is faithful to him and that the children that are produced are his, he will remain with the mother of his children; if a man knows that his wife has been sexually unfaithful to him, marital stability is threatened, and since family and marriage are the nucleus of society,

---
[9] Ibid, pg. 83
[10] Ibid.
[11] Ibid, pg. 192
[11] Ibid.

therefore the stability of all society is threatened, and this is one of the reasons why adultery was seen as a crime in traditional Christendom.

Thomas Acquinas taught that a child is an extension of the parents, meaning a child is an extension of the parent's bodies because they share the same substance as the parents; therefore, the parents are inclined to care for the children, and for the sake of the children and consortium with each other, the parents stay together in marital union.[12] In traditional Christian teachings, marriage is considered a lifelong commitment, not just until children reach maturity but for the entirety of one's life. This is because it is believed that children, in turn, will provide support and care for their parents as they reach old age.[13]

Being an illegitimate child (bastard) in traditional Christendom came with many social stigmas because the child was born out of wedlock, meaning that the child was often born from extramarital unions and pre-marital sex (adultery & fornication), which, if known, became bad for reputation, it was noted on the baptism certificates and property documents.[14] They had numerous problems when it came to inheritance, had numerous problems securing high positions in society, had problems testifying in court, and often suffered poverty and neglect.[15] They were seen as products stemming from immoral acts, and they were often bullied, teased, and discriminated against. Their status gave them problems in accessing

---

[12] Ibid, pg. 85
[13] Ibid.
[14] Ibid, pg. 86
[15] Ibid.

education and healthcare services, and they were often economically disadvantaged because it was difficult to secure financial support from the biological father. Most of these bad stigmas served as a form of social control to deter people from sinful unions.

Traditional Christendom placed strong importance on marriage, family, and fidelity and placed strong condemnation on adultery, fornication, and marital infidelity. Seeing the bad situation of today, illegitimate births and single-parent households place a heavy burden upon society because, without a proper family structure, taxes are used to care for families instead of a strong family unit caring for itself; thus, big government is born.

Traditional Christendom saw rampant fornication as a threat to civilization because if people were free to have random sex with anyone, the human race would turn into savagery because there would be no legitimate bonds between male and female for the care of children, women would become prostitutes, and women would have to solely provide for their offspring, which would coax women into not wanting to have children.[16] Marriage works to provide stability in society for the good of the spouses and children; it is the basic unit of civilization. Christendom outlawed cohabitation without marriage because it diminished the worth of women because it allowed men to gratify their passions without the restraint of marriage, which would also cheapen women; Christendom banned fornication because it is sinful and they wanted to help men and women avoid slipping into

---

[16] Ibid, pg. 292-293

sexual liberty, which was a threat to societal stability and family stability.[17]

Fornication (sex before and outside of marriage) often leads to prostitution, single-parent households, erosion of morals, unwanted children, concubinage, sexually transmitted diseases, relationship instability, emotional and psychological ills, and things against the well-being of spirituality. Adultery was seen as even worse because it came with betrayal. The betrayed spouse would be greatly hurt and lose honor; it brought societal shame, was seen as a moral and religious transgression, disrupted families, brought forth illegitimate children, jeopardized marital vows, spread sin in society, brought forth stigma, etc. As to why traditional Christendom often criminalized fornication and adultery, there were significant moral and religious considerations at play.

---

[17] Witte, J. (2012). *From sacrament to contract: marriage, religion, and law in the Western tradition.* Louisville (Kentucky); Westminster John Knox Press. pg. 298

PATRIARCHY'S INFLUENCE ON STATE AUTHORITY IN TRADITIONAL CHRISTENDOM

When Christendom in Western Civilization is analyzed, it becomes easy to see that it was based upon Kingships and Emperorship in its traditional political structure. In traditional Christendom, the state was often referred to as the commonwealth, yet the family, often referred to as the domestic commonwealth, played an important role in the monarchical structure of Christendom. The domestic commonwealth in traditional Christendom was based upon the absolute authority of the male head of household (paterfamilias), just as the state commonwealth was based on the absolute authority of the king and emperor.[18] As people were used to the authority of the paterfamilias in the family structure, they readily accepted the king as the authority because they were already in obedience to a male head of the household in the home and family.

When the first man, Adam, was on Earth—from the very beginning—the eldest male held the highest authority. Obedience and subjugation fell on all others, and this subjugation was not based on some social contract theory, nor was choice even related in the matter; this obedience is compelled by nature itself.[19] Upon reflection, the hierarchy within the family, with the eldest male having supreme authority over his household, in fact, was replicated in the state,

---

[18] Ibid. 262
[19] Witte, J. (2012). *From sacrament to contract: marriage, religion, and law in the Western tradition*. Louisville (Kentucky); Westminster John Knox Press. pg. 262

the king having supreme authority over the whole state.[20] The father was head of his family, while the king was head of the multitude of families. Just as the father provided land and defended his family, the king would defend and provide for many families.[21] Since obedience to fathers is in the natural law itself, obedience to a king was the same respect as obedience given to a father.[22] This did not mean that the father acted as an authoritarian tyrant over the family; usually, there were agreements made by the partners of the family, but the patriarch often made the leadership and final decision-making of the family.[23]

The family in Roman Christendom was autocratic in nature. The head of the household could be either the father, grandfather, or maybe an uncle; he was given the title of paterfamilias and acted as a petty absolute monarch over his household.[24] The paterfamilias was empowered to make life-death decisions. Any time a new member was introduced to the household, he could decide to accept them; if he did not, the infant, slave, or whoever was abandoned had a chance that he or she may get rescued by an outside actor.[25] Times back then were different from today; another person meant another mouth to feed, and during wartimes and/or times of famine, etc., that extra mouth to feed may have put substantial strain on survival itself.[26] The paterfamilias made sure each family member was observing religion properly; he often acted as a judge over his family, meted out justice, and acted as the boss of the family business.[27]

---
[20] Ibid.
[21] Ibid.
[22] Ibid.
[23] Ibid. pg. 22
[24] Gies, Frances. Marriage and the Family in the Middle Ages (Medieval Life) (pp. 19). HarperCollins. Kindle Edition.
[25] Ibid.
[26] Ibid.
[27] Gies, Frances. Marriage and the Family in the Middle Ages (Medieval Life) (pp. 19). HarperCollins. Kindle Edition

THE FAMILY AS A BUSINESS UNIT IN TRADITIONAL CHRISTENDOM

In traditional Christendom, the family unit often acted as a business unit, where husband, wife, and children worked side by side, supporting the family business, usually children acting as young apprentices.[28] Usually, when the aged parents could no longer run the family business, the businesses were entrusted to the eldest son, who would ensure the business went on and out of duty and use the proceeds to support the parents who no longer could work.[29] Traditional Christendom existed before the Industrial Revolution, and family was the economic basis of the state because, within family households, production happened as far as manufacturing, agricultural, and commercial production was produced.[30]

Furthermore, the family's role as a business unit was deeply intertwined with the religious and moral values of traditional Christendom. The family business was not merely a profit-driven enterprise; it was seen as an extension of the family's commitment to hard work, thrift, and responsible stewardship. These principles, often instilled through religious teachings, emphasized the importance of honest labor and the prudent management of resources. Families were not just producing goods or offering services; they were actively contributing to the welfare of the community and the stability of the state.

---

[28] Ibid, pg. 149
[29] Ibid.
[30] Gies, Frances. Marriage and the Family in the Middle Ages (Medieval Life) (p. 9). HarperCollins. Kindle Edition

This sense of purpose and responsibility was not limited to the family members alone but extended to broader society as well. It was expected that a portion of the profits earned would be dedicated to charitable causes, thus reinforcing the concept of social responsibility. Traditional Christendom's economic foundation, deeply rooted in family businesses, was a testament to the symbiotic relationship between the family, the state, and the Church, where economic prosperity reflected moral values and a means to fulfill religious duties. This family-centric economic model underwent a profound shift with the onset of the Industrial Revolution, challenging the traditional roles and dynamics that had persisted for centuries.

THE FOUNDATIONAL ROLE OF FAMILY IN CIVILIZATION: NURTURING LOVE, PRODUCTIVITY, AND STABILITY

Family is the basis of civilization because it allows a proper partnership between a man and a woman for the proper procreation and upbringing of children that is very moral, pleasant, and useful.[31] It provides an effective and efficient method for pooling resources and the division of labor within the household, fostering a loving and caring relationship between the parents and children.[32] It provides the necessary means for the proper education, nurture, and social development of children in a stable and positive atmosphere. Marriage and the upbringing of children is what keeps civilization going; it's the basis of what

---

[31] Witte, J. (2012). *From sacrament to contract: marriage, religion, and law in the Western tradition.* Louisville (Kentucky); Westminster John Knox Press. pg. 7
[32] Ibid.

drives people to be productive, why land is farmed, and why goods and services are produced. When people work to support a family, for example, they are contributing to civilization while at the same time benefiting their families. When a person goes to work to provide for his family, he produces goods and services for people in return for compensation to provide for his family and benefiting others with his work, thus keeping civilization going. Stable families produce stable people and societies; individual and societal stability fosters a peaceful and tranquil state.[33]

THE VITAL ROLE OF PROCREATION IN SUSTAINING CIVILIZATION

Procreation within the family unit is vitally important for civilization because it is widely agreed upon as one of our biological imperatives to reproduce, to produce a child like unto ourselves with the same or similar nature.[34] It is the very means we, as the human family, produce heirs who will carry on the family name, the next generation to bequeath property to and sustain our lineages throughout the generations.[35] Almost every nation on Earth has its foundations based upon religion, culture, and way of life. Families coming together and reproducing ensures that the nation will live on through the generations.[36] The act of procreation not only ensures the continuity of individual family lines but also plays

---
[33] Ibid, pg. 261
[34] Witte, J. (2012). *From sacrament to contract: marriage, religion, and law in the Western tradition*. Louisville (Kentucky); Westminster John Knox Press. pg. 55
[35] Ibid.
[36] Ibid.

a fundamental role in the preservation of cultural and societal legacies.

Through procreation, families contribute to the collective tapestry of humanity, passing down not only their genetic heritage but also their unique customs, beliefs, and traditions. This intergenerational transfer of cultural knowledge and values is a crucial mechanism for the endurance and evolution of nations. As each new generation emerges, they carry with them the accumulated wisdom of their forebears, strengthening the bonds that tie them to their cultural roots. Furthermore, procreation is a powerful force in uniting larger communities, as it fosters a shared sense of purpose and identity among individuals who collectively contribute to the growth and prosperity of their nation. In this way, procreation serves as a bridge between the past and the future, ensuring that the rich tapestry of human civilization continues to flourish with each passing generation.

Chapter 2:

THE SACRED COVENANT OF MARRIAGE: FIDELITY, OFFSPRING, AND SACRAMENT

In the religious and spiritual sense, marriage has three principal goods: "fidelity, offspring, and sacrament."[37] The world is full of uncleanliness and sin, and marriage provides a way for men and women to live honestly with one another, which enables them to bring up children within the fear of God.[38] It works to provide men and women a legitimate channel to have conjugal relations with one another while at the same time protecting men and women from temptation and sexual immorality due to the weakness of the flesh.[39]

It not only offers a safeguard against sexual immorality but also underscores that within the confines of marriage, sexual morality plays a significant role in the creation of families through the birth of children.[40] Since proper marriage is a sacrament, this type of sanctification of marriage provides sacramental stability within the family and the nation-state.[41] Its purpose is to have a monogamous union between a man and a woman, which

---

[37] Ibid. pg. 81
[38] Ibid. pg. 234
[39] Ibid.
[40] Ibid.
[41] Ibid. pg. 67

is designed from its very nature for the love and support of each other, that both are protected from sexual immorality and temptation and for the religious upbringings of children.[42]

WHAT CONSTITUTED MARRIAGE

For marriage to take place in traditional Christendom, the parties had to be free, usually be both equal in status and class, both consenting, and in almost all cases, the father had to give his daughter in marriage to the husband, while the marriage being publicly celebrated, and then consummated for it to make real and have actual legal effect.[43] The husband usually had to pay the father of a bride payment for the fact that the father was surrendering his authority over his daughter and giving that authority over to the husband, which was called the bride price, along with a dowry being paid to the groom by the bride's family, to ensure marital stability.

Marriage in traditional Christendom was indeed a multifaceted institution, deeply entwined with societal norms and economic transactions. The exchange of bride price and dowry represented financial transactions and symbolized the transfer of familial authority and responsibility from one household to another. The bride's price served as a testament to the husband's willingness to assume the role of protector and provider for his wife, honoring the trust placed in him by the bride's father. Simultaneously, the dowry acted as a safeguard, providing the newlyweds with

---

[42] Ibid, pg. 288
[43] Gies, Frances. Marriage and the Family in the Middle Ages (Medieval Life) (p. 97). HarperCollins. Kindle Edition

economic stability and resources to establish their household. This intricate web of customs ensured not only the legal validity of the marriage but also the continuation of social norms and expectations, reinforcing the significance of family structures in traditional Christendom.

THE SIGNIFICANCE OF MARRIAGE AND PROPERTY IN TRADITIONAL CHRISTENDOM

Marriage was extremely important in traditional Christendom because it was the primary means of property ownership and inheritance.[44] Today's inheritance laws can be tyrannical and easily classified as full-out theft. Today, in the West, a woman could commit adultery out in the clear open and then be empowered by the courts to take, if not all, or a large percentage of the husband's property and money. Can you imagine being a husband, and your wife committed adultery, remarried to the adulterer, getting kicked out of your own house, and ending up paying her alimony and child support?

In the heights of Christendom, property was about an estate attached to the family name to make sure the family name and estate were protected and then to make sure this nobility of the family name was transmitted to the male line by primogeniture (inheritance to firstborn son), and to make sure that genealogy was written down and memorialized.[45] Making sure the family property was preserved and

---

[44] Ibid, pg. 9
[45] Gies, Frances. Marriage and the Family in the Middle Ages (Medieval Life) (p. 218). HarperCollins. Kindle Edition.

protected and passed down to legitimate heirs throughout the generations was to ensure the stability of the family and to make sure family wealth and power were protected and preserved. If property could be easily taken away, fragmented, and broken, the family's wealth and power simply diminish over time. When families have adequate control over property, it works to maintain the family status, influence, and control over their lands, which is equal to freedom and independence.

As the eldest son was able to give proper military service, he was more able to protect his family's property and stand through the use of arms if necessary. Dividing property to multiple heirs created internal family disputes and concentrating resources in the hands of the one male heir often led to more efficient management of those family's resources. Often, the eldest male heir was trained from a young age on managing the family and its resources, which often led to even greater prosperity. Since the eldest male was in power over his family, having the power of the estate and resources only added to his power and influence. Often, noble families owned many acres, and families would live in homes on these acres. Still, the legal power over the lands and resources themselves was controlled by the paterfamilias, a sort of quasi-king over his land and household.

MARRIAGE, DIVORCE, AND PROPERTY: A HISTORICAL PERSPECTIVE

Today, the divorce rate is astonishing. More than half of all marriages today end in divorce, and these are the very same people today who will criticize Christendom for being backward. Fatherlessness today is one of the biggest epidemics of our time. It is agreed by many experts today that fatherlessness is one of the most contributing factors in crime and general immorality. In traditional Christendom, the father was considered the head of his household, empowered with legal powers over his family, and the one who owned the estate and property and had an almost absolute say in its management.

Divorce in Christendom was not simply a moral issue but was heavily focused upon to ensure that family interests and property were protected.[46] Before the Church officially got involved in marriage and divorce, people often got divorced for a multiplicity of reasons. The Church took the position that marriage was, in fact, indissoluble under almost all conditions.[47] If either husband or wife committed adultery, they were still encouraged not to separate but to go in for penance to the Church. The husband or wife, in the case of adultery, if penitent, ought not to separate, and the husband was encouraged not to remarry while she was alive and then take her back as a slave in piety and subjugation.[48]

An adulterous wife was encouraged not to remarry but to wait in "all patient chastity," living on bread

---

[46] Ibid, pg. 11
[47] Ibid.
[48] Ibid, pg. 57

and water alone, doing penance for a year, sleeping alone, and waiting for their spouse to take her back.[49] Even if a husband committed adultery, the woman often could not divorce her husband but was able to permit him to enter a monastery. When marriage was dissolved, it was not dissolved through divorce; it was annulled and treated as if it never existed due to some impediment. They did not believe that adultery broke the sacrament because the adulterous wife or husband could simply do penance and be reconciled again.[50]

During the time of Constantine, he put down rather strenuous restrictions on divorce; he only allowed one party to seek divorce if one party could prove adultery, attempted murder (poisoning), or conviction of a grave crime upon the other party.[51] If a man, for example, wanted to divorce his wife and brought known false charges against her, he was denied the right to remarry; if a woman brought false charges against the husband, she was often denied her dowry and was exiled.[52] At times, emperors allowed for mutual divorce if it was by mutual consent, but both parties retained the property that each party came into the marriage with, and the parties were allowed to remarry; here, property was protected.[53]

The emphasis on restricting divorce during Constantine's time was closely tied to the societal understanding of the family as a fundamental unit of stability. By imposing strict regulations, the state

---

[49] Ibid.
[50] Gies, Frances. Marriage and the Family in the Middle Ages (Medieval Life) (p. 98). HarperCollins. Kindle Edition.
[51] Ibid.
[52] Witte, J. (2012). *From sacrament to contract: marriage, religion, and law in the Western tradition.* Louisville (Kentucky); Westminster John Knox Press. pg. 29
[53] Ibid.

aimed to ensure the longevity of marriages and the preservation of family estates. This approach recognized that divorce could have far-reaching consequences beyond the dissolution of the marital bond, particularly concerning property. The penalties for making false accusations or attempting to exploit the divorce system highlighted the gravity with which these matters were viewed. The measures not only discouraged frivolous divorce but also served as a safeguard against property manipulation. Property rights were considered an essential aspect of marriage, and the protection of individual assets played a crucial role in the legal framework. The historical context reveals that during Constantine's reign, divorce was a complex issue influenced by moral, legal, and economic considerations, reflecting the broader values of the time.

THE SIGNIFICANCE OF CONSENT IN TRADITIONAL WESTERN MARRIAGES

In the Western Tradition, the consent of the father over his daughter in terms of her marriage choice was paramount. There were times when if a person were to marry a woman against the parent's consent, that party who sought the marriage could be excommunicated by the Church.[54] When a potential groom wanted to marry a woman against her parent's parental consent, even if the woman herself consented, it was looked at as a form of abduction, and the laws often declared this union to be invalid, and in some cases, the guilty groom or would-be

---

[54] Gies, Frances. Marriage and the Family in the Middle Ages (Medieval Life) (p. 59). HarperCollins. Kindle Edition.

groom was often sentenced to exile or death on some occasions.⁵⁵

As the Church became more powerful in traditional Christendom, the law codes began to reflect that if parties wanted to marry, they would need the consent of the Church, state, and parents for this marriage to be considered legitimate. Because marriage was not simply based on "love and romance" as in today's standard, marriage had reaching implications for society itself; it was about property, inheritance rights, titles, lands, duties, and responsibilities. When consent was formulated upon these three parties, it ensured societal stability and property, inheritance, titles, and lands were all protected and preserved. When consent upon these three parties was formulated (Church, state, family), it often lessened disputes when it came to inheritance, which, when disputes arose, threatened social order itself.

As marriage was viewed as a sacrament, when the Church got involved and issued its consent and control, it added the necessary spiritual dimension to the marriage and made sure that traditional morality and religious belief governed the marriage, thus ensuring long-term success and stability. Marriage was seen as something far beyond the union of just one man and woman; it was inherently tied to the social fabric of society. Often, parental consent was needed and necessary because the newlywed couple often got economic support from the parents of both

---

⁵⁵ Ibid, pg. 60

sides. They often got a piece of land, a home, and farming necessities to ensure their stability.[56]

THE MORAL AND SOCIAL IMPLICATIONS OF CONTRACEPTION IN CHRISTENDOM

Christendom often viewed any type of contraception to be an evil between married partners because one of the primary purposes of marriage was procreation and children, stemming from the biblical command to be fruitful and multiply; contraception was seen as contrary to the divine command. When married parties engaged in sexual relations with contraception, they were seen as violating the divine law because they were putting their desires over the natural process of procreation. By practicing contraception, they viewed this as the devaluation of the family itself, decreasing the emphasis on procreation, which made people more self-centered on sexuality in terms of pleasure and not procreation.

Because sex was seen as for procreation within the marriage bond, sex outside of marriage (fornication, masturbation, homosexuality, bestiality, etc.) was severely penalized. The punishments for sexual immorality were harsher for clerics over laymen and harsher for men over boys.[57] Most of these sins were dealt with in the penitential aspects of Christendom, and penalties were drawn up to the severity of the offense. But for more grave sexual offenses such as prostitution, sodomy, concubinage, pedophilia, group

---

[56] Gies, Frances. Marriage and the Family in the Middle Ages (Medieval Life) (p. 62). HarperCollins. Kindle Edition.
[57] Ibid. pg. 64

sex, mixed bathing, consortium with slaves, and infanticide, they were often dealt with by the heavy hand of the secular government at the behest and approval of the Church.

THE CHURCH'S ROLE IN MARRIAGE AND FAMILY JURISDICTION

Due to its sacramental nature, the Church eventually took over jurisdiction when it came to marriage and family. When disputes took place, the Church had jurisdiction to resolve disputes when it came to family and marriage. The parish priest had power over the actual marriage ceremony. The priest became the bearer of news of the nuptials taking place and the judge when it came to impediments when an annulment was sought.[58] The reason why the Church eventually took over the jurisdiction of marriage and family was that the early Church Fathers like St. Augustine concluded that marriage is a sacrament and a permanent union between husband and wife, whose primary goods were fidelity, faith, offspring, and a sacred bond not only of two persons but of the whole generational lines of descent.[59]

What made marriage a sacrament between baptized persons is three-pronged: 1. A union between the sexes between them and Christ and the Church, their mutual consent, and the consummation (sexual union).[60] The consummation of the marriage was necessary for the marriage to take legal effect. If the marriage was done but not consummated, it could be

---

[58] Ibid, pg. 219
[59] Ibid, pg. 39
[60] Ibid, pg. 97

dissolved, but once consummated, it could not be dissolved.[61]

When it came to Christians marrying non-believers and pagans, the Church often forbade or strongly condemned these types of marriages due to the call of not being "unequally yoked" with non-believers.[62] Because Jesus clearly spoke out against adultery, even Jesus calling adultery those who divorce their wives and remarry, even calling that a type of adultery, the Church preached to marry those who are single or widowed and forbade people from marrying those who were married or divorced.[63] The Church condemned Christian women from marrying pagans because it led to the "adultery of the soul."[64]

The church also forbade Catholic women from marrying heretics unless or until they accepted the Catholic faith in its orthodoxy.[65] Catholic women were also forbidden to marry Jews because the unity of the faithful was paramount, and a unity between the faithful and the unfaithful brought about disunity of the faithful in traditional Christendom.[66] If parents allowed their daughters to marry a Jew, heretic, or pagan, they often could not receive communion for five years. If parents allowed their daughters to marry a pagan priest, for example, they were forbidden from receiving communion for life and even at the time of death.[67]

---

[61] Ibid, pg. 97
[62] Witte, J. (2012). From sacrament to contract: marriage, religion, and law in the Western tradition. Louisville (Kentucky); Westminster John Knox Press. pg. 57
[63] Ibid, pg. 57
[64] Ibid, pg. 62
[65] Ibid.
[66] Ibid.
[67] Ibid.

FAMILY-BASED LAW ENFORCEMENT AND BLOOD FEUDS IN TRADITIONAL CHRISTENDOM

Traditional Christendom did not have much of a police force or a juvenile detention system. Since the father or eldest male was the paterfamilias of the family, he was empowered to enforce the law within his family. When crimes happened between families, the paterfamilias would usually settle disputes between other paterfamilias of other families. The state rarely got involved in crime and punishment because the paterfamilias was able to settle disputes with relative ease. The only time the state got involved was when the security of the state and/or public order was threatened.[68] Crime was usually treated as a tort, and the family and clan of the person who harmed another wrongfully would facilitate some amends to amend the injured party, usually in the form of payment or compensation.[69]

The state would have to get involved in murder because blood feuds between families could come as a result that could last for decades. An example happened in the sixth century when a husband was rebuked by his brother-in-law for neglecting his wife for loose women. The husband decided not to stop neglecting his wife and pursuing loose women. The brother-in-law then attacked and killed him. Once this happened, the relatives of the murdered husband killed the brother-in-law, and then a giant blood feud began to happen between more distant relatives of the

---

[68] Gies, Frances. Marriage and the Family in the Middle Ages (Medieval Life) (p. 18). HarperCollins. Kindle Edition.
[69] Ibid, pg. 32-33

warring families; it got so bad that most of both families' males were slain on both sides.[70] It got so bad the Frankish queen had to get involved by ordering a type of cease-fire, and when they did not obey, she invited the last of the remaining warring families to a dinner party and allowed them to get drunk, and then ordered her men to decapitate all of them in order to stop the blood feud once and for all.[71]

GENDER ROLES IN TRADITIONAL CHRISTENDOM

In traditional Christendom, mothers focused on nursing and nurturing infant children, while the father and mother would focus on the proper upbringing, education, and discipline of the children.[72] When it came to gender roles, it was based on biblical standards. When the Bible is closely examined, one will find when Eve was created, she was created to be a "helpmeet for Adam" (Gen. 2:18).[73] God placed both Adam and Eve together for the procreation of children. After the fall, God instructed both of them that Adam shall rule over his wife, Eve; therefore, traditional Christendom took on the husband as being head over his wife, and together, both husband and wife were head of the children and that of the entire household.[74]

Since both had different roles to play, each had different duties and roles based on the Bible and natural law to ensure that the household was

---

[70] Gies, Frances. Marriage and the Family in the Middle Ages (Medieval Life) (p. 73). HarperCollins. Kindle Edition.
[71] Ibid.
[72] Witte, J. (2012). From sacrament to contract: marriage, religion, and law in the Western tradition. Louisville (Kentucky); Westminster John Knox Press. pg. 23
[73] Ibid, pg. 258
[74] Ibid.

managed most effectively.⁷⁵ This does not mean the paterfamilias ruled his household as an authoritarian tyrant. He was encouraged to nourish and cherish his wife and household as Christ loves and nourishes the Church.⁷⁶ When he ruled over the wife, he did so benevolently, soberly, chastely, and honestly, along with wisdom and justice.⁷⁷ He was not supposed to be cruel and intolerant, and if he did reproach or admonish her, it was done so benignly in the way of justice and fairness.⁷⁸

The father was also responsible for the spiritual development of his household. He would ensure that his household was up-keeping their religious devotions, doing prayers, Bible reading, and catechization.⁷⁹ He would ensure the discipline of his children, using wisdom in punishment, rebuke, and other forms of discipline, with the sole aim of making righteous children.⁸⁰ The father was the king of his household. In traditional Christendom, the father had more authority than a king in his own household, and the wife was ruler over many things in the household, yet under the headship of the husband.⁸¹

The wife of traditional Christendom was expected to be loving and faithful to the husband and to be wise and prudent in managing the household.⁸² As the scripture teaches, she was expected to show reverence

---

⁷⁵ Ibid.
⁷⁶ Ibid, pg. 259
⁷⁷ Ibid.
⁷⁸ Ibid.
⁷⁹ Ibid.
⁸⁰ Ibid.
⁸¹Witte, J. (2012). From sacrament to contract: marriage, religion, and law in the Western tradition. Louisville (Kentucky); Westminster John Knox Press. pg. 260
⁸² Ibid, pg. 259

to her husband by being submissive to him.[83] She was expected to dress modestly in public, and she was expected to avoid laziness and not be around questionable company that would bring shame and dishonor to the family.[84] She was expected to keep order in her household and ensure that religion was practiced within the household. She would also put extra focus on the daughters and young maidens to instruct them in the ways of traditional Christian womanhood.[85]

The married couple in traditional Christendom were encouraged to act as one flesh, meaning they had to be faithful to each other, help each other, pray together, admonish each other when necessary, serve one another, help each other in attaining salvation, and both were expected to serve God together.[86] They worked together to raise children in the fear of God from the cradle, and they would shame vice and ensure the child was raised in virtue and knew the difference between vice and virtue.[87] They would ensure that each child would be raised to understand a profitable trade to ensure they were able to make a good living to support a future family and carry on the name.

When children grew up, they would counsel them when in courtship in preparation for marriage, and they would take an active role when their children were choosing possible spouses.[88] Because the

---
[83] Ibid.
[84] Ibid.
[85] Ibid.
[86] Ibid, 259-260
[87] Ibid.
[88] Ibid.

parents took so much care of the children, the children owed their parents a lifetime of gratitude, obedience, and reverence, and they would be obliged to take care of their parents when they became elderly and not able to take care of themselves.[89]

In traditional Christendom, women were not simply looked at as a means of having sex and having children. They also possessed skills handed down to them from the prior generations that were extremely beneficial to society, such as making pottery and clothes. They were masters at food preparation and were able to concoct healing remedies for many sicknesses, etc.[90] Women mostly did the "traditional inside the home jobs" such as making butter and cheese, weaving, etc., but they also did some outside jobs like vegetable gardening, gathering, feeding livestock, and along with children, they would help the family farm.[91] The men usually did the "traditional outside work," such as doing farm work, such as plowing, haying, sowing, reaping, etc.[92]

---

[89] Ibid.
[90] Gies, Frances. Marriage and the Family in the Middle Ages (Medieval Life) (p. 34). HarperCollins. Kindle
[91] Ibid.
[92] Ibid.

Chapter 3:

THE EVOLUTION OF DIVORCE AND MARRIAGE LAWS IN TRADITIONAL CHRISTENDOM

Before Cannon law firmly took root in traditional Christendom, the husband could seek divorce for a multiplicity of reasons, from adultery, attempted poisoning, excessive drinking, etc. Historically, the husband had the right to divorce his wife; he did not actually need the family's approval to do it. Getting the family involved was more of a formality.[93] Before Cannon law, the wife could seek divorce if she could prove that her husband deserted her, if he was convicted of high crimes, or if he became a prisoner of war gone for an extended period of time.[94] Usually, when one party sought a divorce, both parties were able to keep the property they came into the marriage with.

In traditional Europe, it was nearly impossible for women to get divorced, but rather easy for men to attain them. When the husband divorced his wife in early Europe, he usually had to make financial amends to the wife's family, to whom she was forced to return after the divorce.[95] It took a different stance

---
[93] I Gies, Frances. Marriage and the Family in the Middle Ages (Medieval Life) (p. 22). HarperCollins. Kindle
[94] Ibid.
[95] Ibid, pg. 33

when it came to Christianity making its way into marriage law. It only allowed divorce for reasons of adultery: "Whosoever shall put away his wife, except it be for fornication, and shall marry another, committeth adultery" (Matthew 19:9). But the early church fathers like St. Augustine and St. Ambrose took on the stance that marriage is indissoluble, meaning they preached that men should not seek a divorce at all, because if a man is married, and seeks a divorce, and married another, as long as the original wife is living, that is considered the crime of adultery.[96]

Divorce was seen as an injustice to women because a woman could put all her faith and effort into a marriage, and when she becomes barren or loses her beauty, a man could simply divorce and marry another; it's an injustice.[97] The problem was if the wife got older, her parents would most likely not be alive at that point, and if she was divorced in her middle age, she would have been stuck with little or no support.[98] It was simply damaging to women to marry them when they are young and beautiful and divorce them when they have reached older age.[99] Although divorce was virtually unheard of in traditional Christendom, separation was frequent. If there was adultery or some type of cruelty that has taken place, Church courts often arranged for formal separations; at times, the wife may leave the home,

---

[96] Ibid, pg. 40
[97] Witte, J. (2012). From sacrament to contract: marriage, religion, and law in the Western tradition. Louisville (Kentucky); Westminster John Knox Press. pg. 86-87
[98] Ibid.
[99] Ibid.

and some type of financial settlement may take place.¹⁰⁰

Even though the Church took the stance that divorce was invalid due to it being indissoluble, it sometimes retreated to positions that there were grounds for divorce, such as adultery, lack of consent, impotence, one person taking holy orders, etc.; often, this was not called a divorce, but an annulment or an impediment. While the Church consistently maintained the position that marriage was indissoluble, it occasionally retreated from this stance to recognize certain grounds for what might be termed a divorce under different terminologies, such as annulment or impediment. These grounds included issues like adultery, lack of consent, impotence, or one person taking holy orders.

This nuanced approach highlighted the tension between the Church's theological ideals and the practical complexities it faced when addressing marital issues. In essence, these instances demonstrated the Church's recognition that exceptional circumstances sometimes warranted a dissolution of the marriage bond, even if it didn't explicitly term it as such. The Church's willingness to acknowledge these grounds reflects its acknowledgment of the complex realities individuals face within the institution of marriage.

---

[100] Gies, Frances. Marriage and the Family in the Middle Ages (Medieval Life) (p. 246). HarperCollins. Kindle

THE ROLE OF CHILDREN IN TRADITIONAL CHRISTENDOM: LEGITIMACY, EDUCATION, AND HEIRSHIP

Children were a prized possession in traditional Christendom. Sons were looked at as the means to multiply the species and a means to preserve the father through his progeny.[101] During these times, they did not send their kids to government-run public schools as it happens today. They would place them under the care of qualified tutors and strongly discourage any type of insolent behavior.[102] Fathers made sure to acquire as much wealth as possible to make sure to put in the inheritance for their sons so that the son would have the means to live a good life and take care of the father when he reached old age.[103] The measure of how much the father loved the son would be how much he took an interest in his education, and if he normally corrected the son through disciplinary measures, that was an act of love, not hate.[104]

Oftentimes, the more noble lineages of Christendom would send their sons to train as knights and daughters to train on social graces.[105] Making sure children would be able to attain a good living was a major duty of the father over the son; oftentimes, children were sent to work with master tradesmen as apprentices, and here, they would work under them to learn respect for authority. Master tradesmen could dish out corporal punishment upon children if they

---

[101] Gies, Frances. Marriage and the Family in the Middle Ages (Medieval Life) (p. 197). HarperCollins. Kindle
[102] Ibid, 203-204
[103] Ibid.
[104] Ibid.
[105] Ibid.

were rude and insolent, which is how they learned. The apprentice had to learn how to restrain his temper; if a master tradesman was unusually cruel, the apprentice was able to submit a grievance to the guild itself for relief.[106]

There was a staunch difference between legitimate and illegitimate children in traditional Christendom. Legitimate children became heirs to the family name, including its property, religion, and lineage.[107] Legitimate children came under the control of the paterfamilias; this control was near absolute, and they could exercise control over their activities, their properties, and even their person until the paterfamilias died or they were given emancipation.[108]

It wasn't just about a power trip; the paterfamilias were responsible for their care, support, and nurture, to facilitate the necessary means for their future marriage and family life and to make sure they could have proper entry into a profession to make a good living.[109] The paterfamilias would also make good provisions for their children in their will and testaments, and legitimate children were considered formal legal members of an extended household under the rule of the paterfamilias.[110]

Illegitimate children, meaning those children born outside of wedlock, children born in adultery, incest, concubinage, etc., did not enjoy the same rights as

---

[106] Gies, Frances. Marriage and the Family in the Middle Ages (Medieval Life) (p. 210). HarperCollins. Kindle
[107] Witte, J. (2012). From sacrament to contract: marriage, religion, and law in the Western tradition. Louisville (Kentucky); Westminster John Knox Press. pg. 26
[108] Ibid.
[109] Ibid.
[110] Ibid.

legitimate children.[111] Oftentimes, men could not support illegitimate children born to concubines, nor were they allowed to leave illegitimate children property in their last will and testaments. Care for illegitimate children most of the time fell upon the mother and her immediate family.

THE TRANSFORMATION OF ADULTERY/FORNICATION LAWS AND MORALITY IN TRADITIONAL CHRISTENDOM

Before Christianity took root in Rome, adultery was mostly only a crime for women. Roman law gave the right for the wronged husband to kill an adulterous wife and lover if caught in the act of adultery.[112] When Constantine came to power and made Christianity the official religion of the Roman Empire, he made adultery an equal crime for both sexes.[113] Adultery was looked at as a major sin and major dishonor because adulterous unions corrupted the blood, disrupted property proceedings and inheritance, and lowered the esteem of the family's legacy and reputation.[114] It was believed that whoever destroys a family is equivalent to destroying the whole human race, and adultery was one act that tore apart families.[115]

Adultery was such a major crime and moral issue that if a husband knew of his wife's adultery and remained with her as if nothing ever happened, he

---
[111] Ibid.
[112] Gies, Frances. Marriage and the Family in the Middle Ages (Medieval Life) (p. 28). HarperCollins. Kindle
[113] Ibid.
[114] Ibid.
[115] Witte, J. (2012). From sacrament to contract: marriage, religion, and law in the Western tradition. Louisville (Kentucky); Westminster John Knox Press. pg. 26

was ordered not to take communion even prior to death. If he lived with her after the fact for some time, he was ordered not to take communion for ten years.[116] Having a wife commit adultery was seen as a pure public disgrace, and before Christianity took root, the adulterous wife had to give up everything she owned, and she could even lose her nose and ears in some cases.[117]

In historical times in Germany, an adulterous wife was publicly humiliated. She could be paraded outside in public with her hair cut off and publicly flogged. Even though she could be beautiful, once dishonored in this way, it would be almost impossible for her to find another husband. In Frankish law, historically, the accused adulterer could be forced into combat until death by the wronged husband.[118] One of the reasons for marriage was to protect the couple from illicit sex because sex within marriage outside procreation was considered a minor sin. In contrast, sex outside marriage (adultery, fornication) was considered a mortal sin.[119] According to the Apostle Paul, total chastity was ideal, yet marriage was also considered good because it promoted stability and order in society; fornication and adultery absolutely overturned the spiritual equilibrium in almost every way possible, and traditional Christendom was staunch against fornication and adultery.[120]

---

[116] Ibid, pg. 21
[117] Gies, Frances. Marriage and the Family in the Middle Ages (Medieval Life) (p. 114). HarperCollins. Kindle
[118] Ibid, pg. 33-34
[119] Witte, J. (2012). From sacrament to contract: marriage, religion, and law in the Western tradition. Louisville (Kentucky); Westminster John Knox Press. pg. 69
[120] Gies, Frances. Marriage and the Family in the Middle Ages (Medieval Life) (p. 97). HarperCollins. Kindle

When it came to fornication and the penalties thereof, it depended on the severity of the offense. Questions were taken into consideration: was the woman a virgin? Was it a neighbor's wife? Was it adultery? Was a child born out of the act? If so, the penance was increased, fines were awarded to the wronged husband, etc.[121] In cases of adultery, both men and women were charged equally, and this crime fell within the jurisdiction of the Church, and fines were often associated with the guilty parties.[122] Once the ecclesiastical court found parties guilty of adultery, at times, there was a temporary forfeit of lands, also with fines, and fines had to be paid to recover the confiscated lands.[123]

Almost every time a married woman engaged in extramarital sexual relations, it was treated as adultery; if done by a married man, it was usually treated as fornication. In these cases, civil and criminal sanctions were pursued against the guilty parties for the crime of adultery.[124] Marriage was seen as being one flesh between the husband and wife, and any type of sinful behavior outside of the one-flesh doctrine was considered prohibited; practices such as sodomy, incest, polygamy, prostitution, and even immoderate dress were considered prohibited because they led to sexual immorality.[125]

---

[121] Ibid, pg. 64
[122] Ibid. 170-171
[123] Ibid, pg. 171
[124] Witte, J. (2012). From sacrament to contract: marriage, religion, and law in the Western tradition. Louisville (Kentucky); Westminster John Knox Press. pg. 27
[125] Ibid, pg. 48

"Know you not that your bodies are the members of Christ? Shall I then take the members of Christ and make them the members of a harlot? God forbid! Or know you not that he who is joined to a harlot is made one body? 'For they shall be,' saith he, 'two in one flesh.' But he who is joined to the Lord is one spirit. Fly fornication. Every sin that a man doth is without the body, but he that committeth fornication sinneth against his own body. Or know you not that your members are the temple of the Holy Ghost, who is in you, whom you have from God: and you are not your own? For you are bought with a great price. Glorify and bear God in your body" (1 Corinthians 6:15-20 (Vulgate).

Taking this verse, it means that if a person would, for example, have relations with a prostitute, he would become united with her in the spiritual sense, and this defiles the body and soul because the Holy Spirit dwells within it. The Apostle Paul taught that celibacy is the best way and that it is better never to touch a woman. He preached that celibacy is best for those who are divorced and widowers but preached that for those who are tempted toward sexual sin, it is "better to marry than to burn," and in marriage, it is lawful for both husband and wife to fulfill each other's sexual needs.[126] But if a woman commits adultery, she puts herself against God's majesty, she injures her husband's reputation by exposing him to shame in the public light, hurts the reputation of the family name and lineage, hurts the reputation of the unborn child

---
[126] Ibid, pg. 49

if there is one, and hurts the already existing children's reputation for life.[127]

There was a major problem with a married man having a concubine on the side because doing this is denying another man a possible partner; instead of being a concubine to an already married man, it would be much better if that woman would be a wife for a single man looking to marry. At times, men who kept a concubine alongside a wife were sometimes flogged, and if a woman was caught in the act of adultery, not only could she be branded with infamia, but she could face expulsion from her town.[128]

Sexual harassment was also a punishable offense, usually resulting in the man who sexually harassed a woman paying fines, and the more the fine increased depended upon the severity of the offense. If a man, for example, fondled a married woman, he would have to pay more than if he fondled a widow.[129] If a woman did something to encourage an advance from another male, the husband often punished her himself, and forms of wife beating took effect.[130]

---

[127] Ibid, pg. 195
[128] Gies, Frances. Marriage and the Family in the Middle Ages (Medieval Life) (p. 155). HarperCollins. Kindle
[129] Ibid.
[130] Ibid.

HOMOSEXUALITY

In the Roman upper classes, before Christianity firmly took root as the official religion of the Empire, the practice of homosexuality among the upper classes was widespread. Once Constantine took power, he made homosexuality an offense that could be given the death penalty as a type of grievous act of fornication.[131] Constantine's crackdown on homosexuality signaled a broader transition from the permissive norms of Roman society to the more conservative and morally stringent principles of Christianity. In this evolving landscape, sexual behavior and morality were central concerns. Same-sex relations, once tolerated among the elite, became a symbol of the old ways, deemed incompatible with the new Christian ethos.

The penalties for homosexuality were severe, reflecting the growing stigmatization of this practice. These legal changes demonstrated the merging of the Church's authority with the power of the Roman state, which sought to enforce Christian moral values through legislation and punishment. This shift marked a critical moment in history when the traditional acceptance of homosexuality began to be replaced by a more restrictive and punitive approach, fundamentally altering the social and cultural landscape.

---

[131] Witte, J. (2012). From sacrament to contract: marriage, religion, and law in the Western tradition. Louisville (Kentucky); Westminster John Knox Press. pg. pg. 29.

THE STAUNCH OPPOSITION TO POLYGAMY IN TRADITIONAL CHRISTENDOM

Traditional Christendom was highly against polygamy, meaning one man and two women at the same time, due to its barbaric nature. If one studies polygamous societies, one will often find savagery taking place. The perfect example of polygamy would be Jacob and Ishmael. It caused rivalries between children born from the same father and different mothers. Roman law especially imposed severe sanctions and penalties upon polygamy.[132]

Polygamy got such a bad reputation in traditional Christendom that it was put alongside the sin of adultery and incest, something considered wicked and unnatural, an offense against God and the State.[133] If a man would, for example, be already married and then marry another while still married to the first, he most likely would have been charged with a type of fornication offense and incur what was called infamia, a type of black mark that prevented one from holding any public office or position of trust and authority within the empire.[134]

If a father allowed or consented to a son getting married in a polygamous manner, he also could suffer the black mark of infamia.[135] For any marriage to take place, there could not be a present marriage already intact, nor could there even be an active engagement; it had to be formally broken off.[136] If a woman

---

[132] Witte, J. (2012). From sacrament to contract: marriage, religion, and law in the Western tradition. Louisville (Kentucky); Westminster John Knox Press. pg. 27
[133] Ibid, pg. 28
[134] Ibid.
[135] Ibid.
[136] Ibid.

consented to a polygamous union, she would suffer the black mark of infamia, but if she was tricked into it, and she could prove it, she could be spared the punishment and save her reputation.[137] As time went on in traditional Christendom, the more the emperors were against the practice of polygamy; eventually, they stopped all Jews from practicing it, and if a Christian were to declare a second wife, all children born to the second wife were declared illegitimate, and the government would seize a portion of the property from practicing polygamists.[138] Eventually, by the time of Emperor Theophilus, he declared polygamy to be a capital crime; thus, it remained a capital crime up until the nineteenth century.[139]

---

[137] Ibid.
[138] Ibid, pg. 28-29
[139] Ibid.

Chapter 4:

MARRIAGE, FAMILY, AND POWER: THE LASTING IMPACT OF THE REFORMATION AND THE FRENCH REVOLUTION

Before the Reformation, the power of the family was very high. Due to factors stemming from the Reformation, the larger kinship/kindred group consisting of the clan kindred/lineage began to lose importance while the power of the state greatly increased.[140] A pattern of history emerges in regard to family and state power in the world: when the government becomes weak or is weak, the supra-family becomes strong or is strong; when the government (secular power) becomes strong or is strong, the family clan or lineage becomes weakened and is greatly weakened in history.[141] Once the sects of Protestantism, Calvinism, and Anglicism were made up, they each formulated a model of marriage and family in the way they saw fit, took jurisprudence away from the Catholic church, and set up their own authorities over it. Each of these sects assigned different authorities: the Lutherans gave authority over marriage and family to the state,

---

[140] Gies, Frances. Marriage and the Family in the Middle Ages (Medieval Life) (p. 296). HarperCollins. Kindle
[141] Ibid.

Calvinists gave it to both, and Anglicans gave it almost exclusively to the church.[142]

How England's political structure formed after the Reformation and the breaking away from the papacy and the Catholic Faith was that family, Church, and state all were subjugated to the king, while the king was subject to God being at the center of the political commonwealth.[143] They created their own archbishop who was not subject to the Pope but to God and king, and the paterfamilias were subject to God, king, and bishop, who stood at the head of the family unit; they believed this was God's natural hierarchy.[144] How this differed from traditional Christendom was that the Pope was supreme in spiritual authority, only subject to God, while emperors and kings were subject to the Pope in spiritual matters, and the paterfamilias was subject to the Pope and to the king who was subject to the papacy.

The major deviation here was the king/emperor became supreme over the papacy, meaning the Pope was no longer the supreme authority over religion. The king became the supreme authority over both the spiritual and material realms. Having the king as supreme over religious matters and not the Pope is one of the biggest deviations in Western history.

---

[142] Witte, J. (2012). From sacrament to contract: marriage, religion, and law in the Western tradition. Louisville (Kentucky); Westminster John Knox Press. pg. 6
[143] Ibid, pg. 266
[144] Ibid.

WHY TRADITIONAL CHRISTENDOM FAVORED CELIBACY AS OPPOSED THE MARRIAGE?

Marriage was looked at not as the optimal state but reserved for those who were tempted by sexual sin because it protected them from committing sexual immorality (adultery, fornication, etc.).[145] Celibacy was idealized because it helped spiritual life by boosting a person's sense of virtue, aided his sense of beatitude, and allowed people to better contemplation.[146] It became an important prerequisite for those serving as clergy and holy orders because that cleric would be working solely for religious service and not to support a family.[147] The idealization of celibacy within the context of Christianity extended beyond its value as a tool against sexual sin. It is also intertwined with the perception of a higher calling.

Celibacy allowed individuals to devote their lives entirely to spiritual service and the Church, free from the responsibilities and distractions of family life. As a result, it became a fundamental prerequisite for those entering the clergy and taking holy orders. By committing to a life of celibacy, the clergy could focus entirely on their religious duties, which included leading the congregation, performing sacraments, and guiding the faithful in their spiritual journeys. This separation of spiritual service from family responsibilities laid the foundation for a distinct and revered class of religious leaders, setting them apart from the laity and emphasizing their unique role in the Christian

---

[145] Ibid, pg. 11
[146] Ibid.
[147] Ibid.

community. This shift in the perception of celibacy as a higher virtue and a means to spiritual service helped shape the structure of the Christian Church and its spiritual leadership for centuries to come.

THE EVOLUTION OF DIVORCE PRACTICES IN THE WAKE OF THE REFORMATION

When Martin Luther started the sect of Protestantism after calling the Pope the anti-Christ, Luther began to make changes in family jurisprudence. The Catholics saw fit to keep marriage indissoluble, while Luther said based on his interpretation of the Bible, that a wife's adultery was sufficient for divorce. Once this was accepted, other justifications for divorce were made up, which included if a woman suffered desertion, severe cruelty, and others.[148] The medieval Catholic church did not overlook things such as adultery, cruelty, etc.; they simply took on the approach that marriage is indissoluble and arranged for agreed-upon separations, which worked as a substitute for divorce.[149]

But as the Reformation was changing the nature of family, the Catholic church maintained that separation is the remedy for divorce. Even if there was separation, the sacramental bond remained between the husband and wife. Neither party was free to marry until the death of the other spouse. The marriage bond simply could not be severed, even if both the husband and wife came out to be condescending toward each other.[150]

---

[148] Gies, Frances. Marriage and the Family in the Middle Ages (Medieval Life) (p. 301). HarperCollins. Kindle
[149] Ibid, pg. 302
[150] Witte, J. (2012). From sacrament to contract: marriage, religion, and law in the Western tradition. Louisville (Kentucky); Westminster John Knox Press. pg. 150

As the Reformation ushered in a new era of thought in terms of marriage and family, the differences in beliefs between Catholics and the emerging Protestant denominations became increasingly apparent. While Luther and other reformers introduced grounds for divorce, the Catholic church remained steadfast in its conviction that marriage was indissoluble, even in the face of issues such as adultery, cruelty, and separation. The Catholic church's stance that separation was a substitute for divorce allowed couples to live apart, but the sacramental bond of marriage remained intact, binding them until the death of one spouse.

This steadfast commitment to the permanence of marriage underscored the Church's belief in the sanctity of the marital bond. While the Reformation brought about significant changes in religious beliefs, it also highlighted the enduring influence of the Catholic church's teachings on the sacredness of marriage. These contrasting views on marriage's indissolubility continued to shape the course of family jurisprudence and marital customs during the Reformation and beyond, creating distinct approaches to the dissolution of marriage between Catholics and Protestants.

LUTHER'S CHALLENGE TO CHASTITY AND CELIBACY IN THE CATHOLIC CHURCH

The Catholic church is known for regarding celibacy as a type of holiness and sanctity, while Luther made celibacy look as if there is no good in it and propagated that marriage and family life are far superior to the celibate life because it protected the idea of property and honor.[151] Luther propagated that the celibate life has no superior virtue over celibacy and that celibacy was not a prerequisite for clerical duties, thus coaxing people into thinking that celibate priests were less virtuous than those who are married and sexually active.[152] To take it a step further, not only did Luther preach against clerical celibacy, but he rejected the laws that ensured clerical celibacy, rejected vows of chastity, etc., and called for clerics to be married.[153]

Martin Luther's stance on celibacy and marriage was indeed a significant departure from the traditional Catholic perspective. Luther argued vehemently that celibacy had no inherent moral superiority over marriage, dismissing the notion that those who remained celibate were holier or more virtuous. He went further by challenging the long-standing requirement of clerical celibacy, asserting that it was not a prerequisite for those in clerical duties. Luther's beliefs were radical for his time, as he openly rejected vows of chastity and the laws

---

[151] Ibid.
[152] Ibid, pg. 6
[153] Witte, J. (2012). From sacrament to contract: marriage, religion, and law in the Western tradition. Louisville (Kentucky); Westminster John Knox Press. pg. 6

enforcing clerical celibacy. Instead, he advocated for clerics to marry, arguing that marriage and family life not only protected property and honor but also allowed priests and ministers to lead fulfilling lives while fulfilling their religious duties. This divergence in views on celibacy and marriage between the Catholic church and Luther's Reformation movement represented a profound shift in the perception of virtue, morality, and duty within the religious context.

LUTHER'S CHALLENGE TO THE SACRAMENT OF MARRIAGE AND ITS IMPACT ON FAMILY LAW AND AUTHORITY

Luther ultimately rejected the idea of marriage as a sacrament because he aimed to establish that marriage was purely a secular institution. By arguing that it wasn't a sacrament, he sought to move it from the authority of the Church to secular jurisdiction. If something is under purely secular jurisdiction, secular authorities can impose their will upon it, but if it's under ecclesiastical jurisdiction, secular authorities have little to no power to alter it or impose their will upon it. He propagated that when marriage was conducted within the Church, it conferred no sanctifying grace upon the husband and wife, as did the other sacraments, such as baptism.[154] Luther persuaded his followers that marriage was simply mostly an earthly doctrine and not a heavenly one, that it was not sacred nor divine, and was intended for

---

[154] Ibid.

mostly secular human interests to serve as strictly human ends and goods.[155]

When it came to marriage being anything in the spiritual realm, he taught that marriage was the best guard against sexual immorality and that it worked to deter sexual immorality such as prostitution, promiscuity, etc.[156] He wanted all fit men to enter this union and to almost completely shun celibacy, even the clerical, which worked as a dagger to the Catholic church. Since he persuaded his followers that marriage was no longer a sacrament and no longer under Church authority because he propagated the "priesthood of all believers," he taught that secular authorities would now act as God's viceregents upon Earth, not the Catholic church, and he put all the authority in the secular powers to enforce all the aspects of marriage, regarding divine and natural laws when it came to family, marriage, and sexual matters.[157]

He still required secular powers to get counsel from religious officials in regard to family and marriage. He taught that pastors were still required to preach to families, but because he propagated the idea that all Christians are all priests (the priesthood of all believers), he saw nothing wrong with secular authorities having jurisdiction over family. His movement ended the Catholic church having formal

---

[155] Ibid.
[156] Ibid.
[157] Ibid.

legal jurisdiction over marriage and family law in Protestant jurisdictions.[158]

Civil marriage courts ended up being created that replaced canon law courts and rules, and Lutheran jurists ended up writing their own jurisprudence regarding marriage and family law, which directly, in many cases, contradicted the Catholic canon law.[159] Because Luther denied marriage as a sacrament, all types of deviations sprung forth, which eventually gave rise to interreligious marriage, all kinds of avenues for divorce, remarriage after divorce, etc.[160] Canon law had impediments against interreligious marriage. While Protestants preached marrying outside the faith was a bad idea, they did not formally prohibit it, and divorces could not go through simply because each party had a different faith.[161]

When the Calvinists split from the Protestants to form a new sect after the new sect of Protestantism, they also taught that marriage was not a sacrament but a type of covenant association between the sexes that belonged to the entire community and not to ecclesiastical jurisdiction.[162] Marriage did not deviate entirely to personal whims after the Reformation; it simply fell from being a sacrament to being based upon contractual and consensual quality and effect.[163] Luther taught that marriage required no prerequisite

---

[158] Witte, J. (2012). From sacrament to contract: marriage, religion, and law in the Western tradition. Louisville (Kentucky); Westminster John Knox Press. pg. 7
[159] Ibid.
[160] Ibid.
[161] Ibid, pg. 173
[162] Ibid.
[163] Ibid, pg. 8

of faith and sanctity, therefore simply being a civil action.[164]

In England, they experimented with Protestant forms of marriage. Yet, it proved to fail, and they rejected and renounced Protestant reforms of marriage and returned it to canon law. Still, with the difference of supreme headship, instead of being under the Pope, they put it under the English Crown as supreme spiritual and secular authority.[165] Heretical Protestants deemed marriage to be earthly in nature and were subject to the prince, not the Pope, and civil law replaced Catholic canon law governing the institution of marriage.

Even though it was subject to the prince and secular power, Church officials were required to give council to the secular powers concerning God's law, and Church powers admonished those who sought divorce or annulment, but the Catholic church lost massive amounts of authority over marriage; it was a massive power grab in Western history.[166] In 1653, England took marriage away from the Church completely and gave it to local justices of the peace, and even had local justices conducting weddings and having complete jurisdiction thereof.[167] Parliament also claimed the power to issue divorces and gave the people the right to remarry after divorce.[168]

Because Luther appealed to the nobility in his writing against the Catholic church, many people of

---

[164] Ibid, pg. 155
[165] Ibid, pg. 9
[166] Ibid, pg. 156
[167] Ibid, pg. 268
[168] Ibid.

nobility were not purely motivated from a pious or religious standpoint but from the standpoint of gaining more power. By taking jurisdiction away from the Catholic church within a country or kingdom, the secular authority now took those powers away from the Catholic church and gained more power themselves. When people began to rebel against the Catholic church, the dagger was taking power away from the Catholic church regarding marriage, and when people were persuaded that marriage was not a sacrament, they gave no or little argument when secular authorities took over the jurisdiction of marriage because it came more into line with people's desires and want for freedom from the canon law. When they accepted that marriage was not a sacrament, they also easily accepted that marriage was dissolvable and not a permanent union, dissolving upon the death of one of the parties as canon law taught.[169]

In response to the rising challenges associated with premarital sex, pregnancy, and private promises of marriage, the Protestants faced a complex situation in dealing with issues of marriage and family law. To address these challenges, they implemented various measures under government coercion. These measures included compelling individuals to officially register their marriages with local Church clerics, ensuring that marital engagements were publicly announced within the community, and requiring parental consent as a vital component of the marriage process. Additionally, the authorities were forced to take more severe actions, such as imprisoning

---

[169] Witte, J. (2012). From sacrament to contract: marriage, religion, and law in the Western tradition. Louisville (Kentucky); Westminster John Knox Press. pg. 130

individuals who consummated marriages before a Church ceremony.

In some cases, individuals were banished from their communities, and they faced excommunication from the Church, all in an effort to enforce the newly established marriage and family regulations. These stringent measures aimed to regulate and monitor the institution of marriage, ensuring that it aligned with the moral and religious standards set by the Protestant authorities.

CHALLENGING TRADITIONAL HIERARCHIES AND GENDER ROLES IN THE WAKE OF THE REFORMATION

Since kings could now be beheaded for abuses against the nation, Protestants began to challenge the authority of the paterfamilias. This marked a significant shift in traditional hierarchies as power dynamics within families came under direct scrutiny. The conventional structure, where the husband ruled over the wife, both parents held authority over their children, and the paterfamilias could not be easily deposed, even for reasons of abuse within the household, faced growing opposition. The emerging Protestant ideals fostered discussions and debates regarding the balance of power within families as individuals began to question the unchecked authority of the male head of the household.

These conversations about family dynamics contributed to broader discussions of authority, accountability, and justice, which were pivotal in shaping the evolving landscape of marriage, family life, and societal structures during this period of transformation.

During and after the Reformation, evolving perspectives on gender roles began to challenge traditional norms. As Protestant ideas spread, there was a growing emphasis on individual spiritual connection and personal interpretation of religious texts. This shift in religious thought led to a reevaluation of gender roles within families. While traditional Christendom had firmly established male dominance and female submission in marriage and society, Protestantism introduced a more egalitarian perspective. Many reformers, including Martin Luther, emphasized the priesthood of all believers, extending spiritual equality to both men and women. Women like Katharina von Bora, who later married Luther, played influential roles in their households and communities. This movement toward a more balanced view of gender roles marked a significant departure from traditional norms, laying the foundation for the ongoing evolution of gender dynamics that would continue in the centuries to come.

THE CATHOLIC SACRAMENTAL MODEL OF MARRIAGE AND ITS THREEFOLD PURPOSE

The Catholic Sacramental model of marriage was and is based upon Jesus saying, "Whoever shall put away his wife, except it be for fornication, and shall marry another, committeth adultery" (Matthew 19:9). By allowing divorce, it represented divine infidelity, and the Church opposed its practice.[170] The Catholic church instead promoted separation from bed and board in place of divorce because the bond could never be broken, even if both the husband and wife stay away from each other for the rest of their lives.[171]

The early church fathers, such as St. Augustine of Hippo, taught that marriage is a God-given institution that served three distinct purposes: 1. Fidelity, 2. Sacramental stability, and 3. Serving the goods of children.[172] Catholic writers, over time, treated marriage in three district forms: 1. Natural, 2. Sacramental, and 3. Contractual.[173] The natural part is based upon God's command to be fruitful and multiply, to properly raise children, and serve as a shield for lust, that one's sexual behavior falls within marriage that serves the purposes of community and Church instead of sexual immorality, which serves no legitimate purpose.[174]

The contractual part is about a union between husband and wife based upon mutual consent, which

---

[170] Witte, J. (2012). From sacrament to contract: marriage, religion, and law in the Western tradition. Louisville (Kentucky); Westminster John Knox Press. pg. 256
[171] Ibid.
[172] Ibid, pg. 4-5
[173] Ibid.
[174] Ibid.

prescribes a lifelong commitment to each other alongside certain duties and commitment to each other and to offspring that is produced within the union.[175] Finally, it is sacramental in that it becomes an indissoluble union between the husband and wife and between Christ and the Church, conveying sacramental grace upon them.[176] The sacrament of marriage sanctified the couple because they married under God's law and submitted to God's form of ideal marriage in Christ while sanctifying their children because the children become legitimate members of Church, state, and the commonwealth.[177]

The children become legitimate members of the Church and society by the parents nurturing and teaching them to be the next generation of Church parishioners.[178] Once the husband and wife come together under the sacrament of marriage, it works to spiritually transform the marriage, removing sin from sexual intercourse and facilitating righteous procreation. God offers divine assistance in both parents' parental duties. At the same time, the Church nurtures and teaches Catholic believers, and the now-married couple can pass that same nurture and education down to their children, enabling the entire household to be righteous.[179]

---

[175] Ibid.
[176] Ibid.
[177] Ibid, pg. 92
[178] Ibid.
[179] Witte, J. (2012). From sacrament to contract: marriage, religion, and law in the Western tradition. Louisville (Kentucky); Westminster John Knox Press. pg. 93

THE INFLUENCE AND REGULATIONS OF CATHOLIC CANON LAW ON MARRIAGE AND FAMILY

The Catholic canon law outlawed certain practices that it deemed harmful to marriage and family, whether that was punishing and outlawing contraception, sodomy, fornication, adultery, immodest dress, abortion, incest, buggery, bestiality, polygamy, and cruelty or abuse to children and wives.[180] It promoted virtuous and pious behavior that led to chastity and modesty by calling for modesty in dress and separating the sexes in educational institutions and public bathing houses.[181] The Catholic canon law was the source of family law that governed all of Christendom, and it became the law of the entire West; it held supreme authority in Christendom until the Reformation.[182]

During Christendom, the Church had vast jurisdiction over multitudes of peoples and things, from education, inheritance, moral crimes, marriage, etc., which was based upon Jesus giving the keys to Peter (Matthew 16:18-19).[183] The canon law was so successful in Christendom that it governed marriage almost exclusively in all Christendom from the years 1200-1500 AD.[184]

Even though divorce was not possible in the canon law, certain impediments could be brought up, such as being below the age of consent, being already

---

[180] Ibid, pg. 5
[181] Ibid, pg. 60
[182] Ibid, pg. 97
[183] Ibid.
[184] Ibid, pg. 98

married, if the union was based on incest, disease, or some type of deformity, heresy, etc., if anyone of these impediments were proven, the Church through the canon law could annul the marriage.[185] For many years, the canon law viewed a legitimate marriage when a couple promises to marry in the future and then follows that promise with sexual intercourse, which consummates the marriage.[186] This form of marriage eventually was seen as a problem because fornication was a punishable offense, and without the promise of marriage, intercourse here can easily be seen as fornication.

Eventually, during the Council of Trent, the church prescribed that marriages must be contracted in a Catholic church with a priest in the presence of witnesses, and failure to comply with this prescription was often severely punished.[187] The parties that got married had to record their names and witnesses in the local parish register for the marriage to be legitimate, and if people did not go through the Church and the priest, the marriage was deemed null and void, and certain penalties would be prescribed to the parties who attempted to contract a marriage outside the Church.[188] The Catholic canon law forbade Catholics to marry non-Christians or heretics and also forbade Christians from marrying Pagans and Jews.[189]

---

[185] Ibid, pg. 99-100
[186] Ibid, pg. 100
[187] Ibid, pg. 107
[188] Witte, J. (2012). From sacrament to contract: marriage, religion, and law in the Western tradition. Louisville (Kentucky); Westminster John Knox Press. pg. 107
[189] Ibid, pg. 101

MARRIAGE IN THE ENLIGHTENMENT ERA

The Enlightenment was an intellectual and philosophical movement that emerged in the late 17th and 18th centuries, emphasizing reason, individualism, and the pursuit of knowledge through scientific inquiry and critical thinking. It promoted ideas of liberty, tolerance, and human rights, challenging traditional authority and religious dogma. In the context of family law in Christendom, the Enlightenment had a profound impact by promoting the principles of individual rights and secularism, which began to challenge the authority of religious institutions over matters of marriage and family. It contributed to the eventual separation of Church and state in legal matters, paving the way for more secular approaches to family law and individual freedom within marriages.

As time went on after the Reformation, after the break from the Catholic church, and after the people began to believe that marriage was not a sacrament, and therefore putting it under secular authority and jurisdiction, marriage further deteriorated. Marriage devolved into a state of being that people no longer wanted to be bound by God, nature, church, state, tradition, or what is best for the community in terms of marriage. They sought marriage rules and norms to be made up by the marriage parties themselves; freedom was given to the people to make marriage as they saw fit.[190] Instead of God's will and the Church's will, the wills of the married parties became paramount

---

[190] Ibid, pg. 11

in the new "enlightenment era," and neither the Church nor the community, not even the paterfamilias of the family, could override the will of the private parties upon the marriage they contracted.[191]

Today, this type of ideology concerning marriage has descended into absolute chaos, with pre-nuptial contracts, God and religion out of marriage, no-fault divorce, etc., nearly 50 percent of all marriages end in divorce. It is so bad today that nearly one-quarter of all pregnancies in America today are aborted. In the black community, nearly two-thirds of all children are raised without fathers, and single mothers are much more likely to face serious financial burdens, such as poverty and bankruptcy.[192] It is proven that many children raised in broken homes often suffer from behavior problems, are more likely to be abused, and are more likely to end up being criminals.[193] When a marriage breaks down, it is not men who suffer; the major burdens usually fall upon women and children.[194]

---

[191] Ibid.
[192] Ibid, pg. 321
[193] Ibid.
[194] Ibid.

HOW THE FRENCH REVOLUTION SHAPED FAMILY AND MARRIAGE IN THE WEST

The French Revolution, which began in 1789, was a pivotal period in French history characterized by a series of political, social, and economic upheavals. It sought to dismantle the absolute monarchy, challenge the aristocracy's privileges, and establish the principles of liberty, equality, and fraternity. The revolution witnessed significant events, including the storming of the Bastille, the Reign of Terror, and the rise of Napoleon Bonaparte. The revolution had a profound impact not only on Francebut also on the wider world, as it influenced subsequent revolutionary movements and the development of modern political ideologies. Regarding changes in how family was governed, the French Revolution had a notable impact on family structures and law.

The revolutionaries aimed to replace the old feudal and ecclesiastical systems with more egalitarian and secular principles. They introduced significant changes to family governance, including the dissolution of religious control over marriage and the establishment of civil marriage, allowing for greater individual choice. The revolution also sought to reduce the influence of the aristocracy in family matters and promote legal equality within families. Additionally, inheritance and property rights laws were reformed to align with the principles of equality and the nation's interests. These changes laid the groundwork for modern family and civil laws in France, which continue to influence family governance to this day. The overall theme of the French Revolution regarding family overturned the traditional views and ideologies of family and marriage while promoting secularism, equality, and liberty in family, marriage, and raising children. The major reason why enemies of tradition sought to overturn the traditional family structure was that they were trying to overturn the monarchy and the classical system because they saw that patriarchy, meaning the father having the power of a king over his family, as being correlated with a monarch having rule over a kingdom; because people accepted the paterfamilias within the household, they naturally accepted the king over the entire kingdom.

The paterfamilias did not govern his family based on choice or the consent of the governed. It was in fact believed to be ordained by God, and this belief also extended to the king ruling over the kingdom as ordained by God, and not by some type of social contract or consent of the governed.[195] Monarchs made sure to reinforce fatherly authority within the household and made sure to facilitate the stability of families, especially the noble lineages of his elite allies.[196] Monarchs defended the Christian notion of marriage being indissoluble. They sought to criminalize adultery, not allow illegitimate children to inherit and have equal civil status to legitimate children, and facilitated the paterfamilias of family households to be able to imprison rebellious children

---

[195] Desan, S., & University Of California Press. (2004). The family on trial in revolutionary France. University Of California Press, Berkley and Los Angeles, California, pg. 1
[196] Ibid, pg. 2

and adulterous wives to reinforce the power of the paterfamilias which worked to ensure kingly power.[197]

One of the first actions of the new secular government that formed after the Reformation and during and after the French Revolution was to dismantle the traditional family structure to free the household from the paterfamilias and give liberty and civil rights to family members who were once under the paterfamilias.[198] They allowed divorce, redefined marriage as only a civil contract, made inheritance egalitarian, and greatly reduced the power of the father within the household, thus birthing a big secular government.[199] They forced illegitimate children into the family with legitimate children, and they completely secularized marriage, took record keeping away from the Church, and gave it to civil secular authority.[200]

Since the people now elected the state's rulers, they argued that marriage should be based on the free choice of people.[201] They completely dismantled the notions of the indissolubility of marriage, promoted that celibacy was a worthless endeavor, dismantled parental authority over marriage, overturned the dowry system, and dismantled most any law stemming from the canon law.[202] They took nearly all the power away from the father of the household because they wanted to promote equality and dismantle hierarchy and tradition. The paterfamilias

---
[197] Ibid.
[198] Desan, S., & University of California Press. (2004). The family on trial in revolutionary France. University Of California Press, Berkley and Los Angeles, California, pg. 4
[199] Ibid.
[200] Ibid.
[201] Ibid, pg. 15
[202] Ibid.

had so much power over his family in traditional Christendom that the father was able to imprison his wife and children for disobedience or adultery on behalf of the wife.

Here, the powers during the French Revolution stripped the father of this power and attempted to take religion almost completely out of marriage. Religion was frowned upon because it represented superstition and tradition that a marriage was legitimate only if the couple conducted a civil marriage prior to a religious marriage.[203] They believed the freedom of the heart was the foundation of all happiness, not marriage being a sacrament of the Catholic church.[204] They preached that easy divorce would make marriage happier because men would be incentivized to treat women better because they could divorce them if they wanted to or if the husband treated them badly.[205]

They did away with the paterfamilias being in control of family property and promoted equality in control of property. They eliminated dowries because they believed marriages would be strengthened based on personal charm, more so than having wealth and offering a big dowry.[206] They did away with parents having authority over children's marriages, lowered the age of consent, took all power away from the Church regarding marriage and family, established secular courts for marriage and divorce, and took record keeping away from the Catholic church and clerical control which recorded marriages, births,

---

[203] Ibid, pg. 29
[204] Ibid, pg. 35
[205] Ibid, pg. 39
[206] Ibid, pg. 41

divorces, and deaths.[207] They propagated that marriage was a civil contract formulated by the parties they could dissolve, free from all religion, spirituality, and anything associated with the divine.[208] Traditional marriage was based upon the wife owing fidelity and submissiveness to the husband and the husband owing protection, help, and a marital home to the wife, yet the French Revolution sought to overturn that for egalitarian and secular principles.[209]

They overturned the law that only allowed Catholics to marry other Catholics and allowed for interreligious marriage, for example, allowing a Christian to marry a Jew or a Protestant.[210] They were so against religion and so threatened by it that they made clergy take an oath of fidelity to the new secular nation and constitution.[211] Instead of a king ruling over his kingdom, the state now worked to protect the individual liberty of the citizens against what they believed to be the tyranny of monarchy and paternal power. The power of the father was simply taken away, and he lost the ability to arrange marriages for his children. The fatherly rule was taken away for the social aspects of egalitarianism.[212]

For centuries, the paterfamilias would practice entailment or substitution in terms of property and inheritance, which meant that the paterfamilias could restrict inheritance to a specific line of succession to ensure that their legacies would descend in their

---

[207] Ibid, pg. 49
[208] Ibid.
[209] Desan, S., & University Of California Press. (2004). The family on trial in revolutionary France. University Of California Press, Berkley and Los Angeles, California, pg. 49
[210] Ibid, pg. 52
[211] Ibid, pg. 53
[212] Ibid, pg. 61

specific lineages, to pass down estates, lands, and titles to their specific lineage. The paterfamilias were empowered to establish legal restrictions to how property is inherited to protect property so it does not get fragmented and to ensure that the power of the family, lineage, and property are preserved and protected through the generations. This practice kept families wealthy and noble; often, conditions were laid out that the inheritors had to meet to inherit the property; this worked to ensure the property would not be sold and transferred to others.

Here, the secular authorities of the French Revolution abolished this practice to cancel out the power of the father.[213] Then, the secular authorities further put a dagger into the paterfamilias by abolishing the practice of primogeniture, which was a traditional practice that the firstborn son would inherit the entire or larger portion of the estate, property, and/or titles.[214] The wisdom of primogeniture was that it enforced the power of the paterfamilias, which worked to keep the property, power, and wealth within the family, especially noble families; this also worked to stop fragmentation of property and consolidated all that power within the hands of a single heir, typically the eldest son, who would have the power to ensure that the family legacy goes on in spirit and letter; here the new secular authorities almost completely gutted this system to end the paterfamilias and bring about secularism.

---

[213] Ibid, pg. 62
[214] Ibid, pg. 233

Many historians make the rationale that the power of the paterfamilias was the source of the absolutist monarch in traditional France because they believed the authority of kings was linked to the household power of fathers; if people accepted the power of the paterfamilias, they would easily accept the power of a king. Furthermore, the paterfamilias would preserve family legacy by requesting lettres de cachet (sealed letters), which were mechanisms to preserve family honor by keeping daughters from unsuitable relationships to punish sons who showed insolence and disobedience.[215] Here, these letters were sealed by the king's seal, which worked to imprison individuals without trial or due process.

Here, the paterfamilias could request them to imprison disobedient or adulterous wives and disobedient children, reinforcing the paterfamilias' power and authority over his household. Here, he could imprison adulterous wives and children who needed to be disciplined. He would, for example, imprison his daughter, who sought a marriage or sexual union that went against family honor to protect property, religion, and lineage and to prevent family scandal if needed.

The imprisoned family members often went into a convent, monasteries, or private facilities, and the paterfamilias determined the time the person had to serve. When kings used this power, people often complained that it was an abuse of power, which was one reason why people revolted against the monarch. During the French Revolution, they abolished lettres de

---
[215] Ibid, pg. 143

cachet as a blow to the monarchy and the paterfamilias to help usher in secularism. After abolishing the power of the father regarding disciplining his children, the new secular government set up family arbitration courts to deal with problem children. The secular government took over disciplining children and destroyed the power of the fathers.[216]

Then, the new secular government went after the condemnation of illegitimate children and began to grant rights to illegitimate children by offering welfare for unwed mothers of illegitimate children. Later, if recognized by parents, illegitimate children were able to inherit equally with legitimate children.[217] The problem with this is that marriage was based upon the wife's fidelity because if the father is certain the children are his, the father would provide the means of care of his wife and family; because the children are products of the fatherhood, they were the ensured lineage of the father; the paterfamilias.[218]

When there was confusion about the paternity of children, it created scandal, confusion, and chaos regarding raising children and the stability of families. There is no greater insult to a man than knowing he was raising another man's offspring, thinking they were his own; if a wife committed adultery, the man would forever question whether the children are really from his own loins; this is why adultery was considered a criminal offense. The essence of marriage in traditional Christendom was the wife's

---

[216] Desan, S., & University Of California Press. (2004). The family on trial in revolutionary France. University Of California Press, Berkley and Los Angeles, California, pg. 146
[217] Ibid, pg. 179
[218] Ibid, pg. 210

fidelity because it ensured with certainty the paternity of the children, which reinforced and maintained the trust of family property.[219]

Here, the secular authorities put single mothers with illegitimate children under state care with state pensions in state homes, and the illegitimate children became children of the nation.[220] Illegitimate children were threats because they would compete with legitimate children over property that rightfully belongs to them by marriage between parents; if illegitimate children were able to inherit, that would promote savagery because a society of illegitimate children creates crime, promoting instability.[221]

Family lineage and property passed down to legitimate heirs worked as the building block of stable social structure, which gave birth to orderly societies by changing the status of illegitimate children, promoting egalitarian inheritance, allowing children to be defiant toward family plans of marital and succession planning, taking away paternal authority, and allowing for easy divorce, destroyed societal stability.[222] If a wife committed adultery, it simply dissolved the family, and easy divorce deprived the man of his most sacred property, his family. Traditional Christendom reinforced the power of the husband to prevent foreign children into the family, and a wife's adultery and infidelity could create property disputes and misdirect property.[223]

---

[219] Ibid, pg. 241
[220] Ibid, pg. 213
[221] Ibid, pg. 242
[222] Desan, S., & University of California Press. (2004). The family on trial in revolutionary France. University Of California Press, Berkley and Los Angeles, California, pg. 252, 263
[223] Ibid, pg. 304

ST. JOHN CHRYSOSTOM ON CHRISTIAN MARRIAGE: BIBLICAL FOUNDATIONS, BISHOP'S ROLE, AND CATHOLIC TEACHINGS ON FAMILY LIFE

He taught that family had everything to do with the bishop (successors of the apostles) of your diocese, meaning that if Christians wanted to marry, they must get the bishop's permission because St. Ignatius said: "It is right for men and women who marry to be united with the consent of the bishop, that marriage be according to the Lord and not according to lust."[224] He taught that the scriptures taught against polygamy and fornication because of this biblical verse: "It is well for a man not to touch a woman. But because of the temptation to immorality, each man should have his own wife and each woman her own husband" (1 Corinthians 7:1-2).

Marriage is a union that turns both husband and wife into one flesh. This calls that both husband and wife serve each other, that the actual body of each of the husband and wife become the property of the other, as in if a prostitute tries to seduce a married husband, he is to tell the prostitute this is not my body, but my wife's, and vice versa if a stranger is trying to undermine a wife's fidelity.[225] He taught that husbands and wives should not abstain from sexual relations with each other without the consent of either party because this is how adulteries and fornications end up happening.[226] He reinforced the biblical teachings for wives to be submissive to their husbands. He taught as the Bible teaches that men are

---

[224] Chrysostom, J., Roth, C. P., & Anderson, D. (1986). *On marriage and family life*. St. Vladimir's Seminary Press, pg.12
[225] Ibid, pg., 26-27
[226] Ibid, pg. 27

the head of the wife as Christ is the head of the Church.[227] He reinforced the epistles to Paul that said the husband is the leader and provider while the wife's principal duty is submission.[228]

CONCLUDING TEACHINGS ON THE CATECHISM OF THE CATHOLIC CHURCH AND THE CANON LAW REGARDING MARRIAGE AND FAMILY

The purpose of marriage, according to the Catechism, is that the man and woman establish themselves in the marital bond for the whole of life, for the good of the spouses, and for the procreation and proper education of the children that come out of the marital bound; it is a covenant between baptized person's that raises it to the level of a sacrament.[229] It is based upon the ideology of the New Testament regarding marriage that reads: "What therefore God has joined together, let no man put asunder" (Matthew 19:6), "For this reason a man shall leave his father and mother and be joined to his wife, and the two shall become one" (Genesis 2:24),

"Whoever divorces his wife and marries another, commits adultery against her, and if she divorces her husband and marries another she commits adultery" (Mark 10:11-12). Marriage is based on the procreation of children and the mutual help and "remedy of concupiscence"; the mutual help between the spouses and the procreation of children are equal in importance.[230] This mutual help between the spouses

---

[227] Ibid, pg. 43
[228] Ibid.
[229] Catholic Church, & Libreria Editrice Vaticana. (1994). Catechism of the Catholic Church: revised in accordance with the official Latin text promulgated by Pope John Paul II. Libreria Editrice Vaticana, pg. 400
[230] Orsy, L. M. (1990). Marriage in canon law : texts and comments, reflections and questions. Liturgical Press, pg. 46-47

is about tending to the spiritual, emotional, and physical needs of the spouses and consortium as a lifelong commitment. Catholic marriage as a sacrament has the elements of a spiritual union, emotional and psychological bonds, fidelity between the spouses, and indissolubility.

FURTHER INSIGHTS INTO ST. JOHN CHRYSOSTOM'S TEACHINGS ON THE BISHOP'S ROLE IN CHRISTIAN MARRIAGE

St. John Chrysostom's teachings placed significant emphasis on the role of the bishop in Christian marriages, drawing from both the Apostolic tradition and Scripture to reinforce his views. He believed that marriage within the Christian community was not a merely secular or private arrangement, but rather, a sacred institution that should be overseen by the Church. This idea, rooted in the early Christian tradition, was echoed by St. Ignatius of Antioch, who stated that "It is right for men and women who marry to be united with the consent of the bishop, that marriage be according to the Lord and not according to lust." The bishop, as the successor of the Apostles, was entrusted with the spiritual welfare of the faithful, including overseeing the sanctity of marriages within his diocese.

This oversight was not merely ceremonial but intended to ensure that the marriage followed Christian principles, particularly in avoiding the sins of lust, fornication, and polygamy. By placing marriage under the authority of the bishop, St. John Chrysostom highlighted the responsibility of the

Church to safeguard the integrity of Christian family life, making marriage a reflection of the relationship between Christ and His Church. In this context, the family became an extension of the Church, a domestic church in its own right, where both spiritual and physical unions were sanctified under the bishop's guidance.

Furthermore, Chrysostom's view that marriage required the bishop's consent emphasized the communal and sacramental nature of marriage. It was not a private contract, but a public witness to God's grace and a vital component of the Christian life. The approval of the bishop acted as a safeguard, ensuring that the union was entered into with proper understanding and spiritual maturity, in alignment with the teachings of the Gospel.

THE SACRED BOND OF MARRIAGE AND MUTUAL SUBMISSION

In line with biblical teachings, Chrysostom reinforced the idea that marriage is a union in which husband and wife become "one flesh" (Genesis 2:24). This sacred bond required that both spouses serve each other selflessly, mirroring Christ's relationship with the Church. He interpreted the apostle Paul's teaching in 1 Corinthians 7:1-2—"It is well for a man not to touch a woman. But because of the temptation to immorality, each man should have his own wife and each woman her own husband"—as a call to fidelity and exclusivity in marriage. Chrysostom's understanding was that the bodies of husband and wife are no longer their own, but belong to each other.

This reciprocal ownership was essential in maintaining the purity of marriage. For example, Chrysostom warned against the temptation of adultery by teaching that if a man or woman were approached by a stranger seeking to seduce them, they must declare that their body is not their own but belongs to their spouse. This profound sense of mutual belonging and respect formed the cornerstone of marital fidelity and chastity. Chrysostom's teachings warned against any form of abstinence from sexual relations between spouses without mutual consent, as he believed this could lead to adultery or fornication, undermining the sanctity of the marital bond.

Moreover, Chrysostom emphasized the biblical principle of submission in marriage, particularly focusing on St. Paul's instruction that wives should be submissive to their husbands as the Church is to Christ (Ephesians 5:22-24). For Chrysostom, this hierarchy within marriage was not one of domination but of order and love. Just as Christ lovingly leads the Church, so too must the husband lead his wife, providing for her spiritual and temporal needs. In turn, the wife's submission is an act of love, reflecting the harmony and mutual respect that should define the marriage.

Chrysostom also noted the importance of the husband's role as a leader and protector within the marriage, ensuring the family's spiritual well-being. His teachings aligned closely with the Apostle Paul's exhortation that men must love their wives "as Christ loved the Church and gave himself up for her" (Ephesians 5:25). This sacrificial love, according to Chrysostom, ensured that the husband's leadership would be grounded in humility and devotion, rather than power or dominance. The wife's submission, therefore, was not about inequality but about the proper order established by God for the spiritual flourishing of the family.

FURTHER INSIGHTS INTO MARRIAGE IN THE LIGHT OF CANON LAW AND THE CATECHISM OF THE CATHOLIC CHURCH

The teachings of St. John Chrysostom on marriage find their reflection in the Catholic Church's Canon Law and the Catechism, which emphasize the sacramental nature of marriage and its indissolubility. According to the Catechism of the Catholic Church, marriage is more than a legal contract—it is a covenant that binds a man and woman for life. This covenant is rooted in the biblical teaching that "What therefore God has joined together, let no man put asunder" (Matthew 19:6). In marriage, the spouses commit to a lifelong partnership that serves not only their personal good but also the greater good of their family and the Church.

Canon Law outlines the requirements for a valid marriage, emphasizing that the mutual consent of the spouses is necessary for the sacrament to be valid. This consent must be freely given and is a reflection of their total self-gift to one another, which mirrors the self-giving love of Christ. Furthermore, the Church teaches that the primary purposes of marriage are the procreation and education of children, alongside the mutual help of the spouses. In this way, marriage serves both the personal fulfillment of the couple and the continuation of God's creative work through the generation of new life.

In the eyes of the Church, marriage is indissoluble. Once a valid sacramental marriage has been consummated, it cannot be dissolved by any human power. The Catechism also highlights the importance of fidelity within marriage, reflecting the faithfulness of Christ to His Church. This fidelity is not only physical but also emotional and spiritual, as the spouses grow together in holiness, helping each other along the path of salvation.

The Church's teaching on marriage stands in stark contrast to the secular view of marriage as a temporary or contractual relationship. For Catholics, marriage is a sacred institution that reflects God's eternal covenant with humanity. It is a lifelong commitment that requires love, sacrifice, and mutual respect, with the ultimate goal of leading both spouses to heaven.

Conclusion

The traditional Christian perspective on family, marriage, and fidelity has profoundly impacted societal values and governance. Family was seen as the building block of society, essential for transmitting property, religion, culture, and heritage from generation to generation. Stability within the family was intertwined with the stability of society. Fidelity in marriage was promoted as a means of maintaining this stability, while adultery and fornication were viewed as threats to both family and societal cohesion. These transgressions led to issues such as illegitimate births, single-parent households, and the erosion of moral values. Traditional Christendom's moral and legal stance on family and fidelity reflected broader concerns for preserving family unity, social order, and moral rectitude. While modern society has seen shifts in its approach to family and marriage, the historical perspective remains a significant part of the conversation around these values.

Patriarchy's influence on state authority in traditional Christendom is a captivating historical perspective, illustrating the interconnectedness of family and state. The paterfamilias, as the head of the family, mirrored the monarchical structure of the state, exercising authority over life, religion, justice, and family businesses. The family also functioned as an economic unit, with members, including children, working together to support the household. This structure underpinned the state's stability, as the family's economic role was central to society. The close relationship between family and state governance highlights the family's role not only as a social institution but as a key contributor to the economic and political framework of Christendom.

In traditional Christendom, the family was also viewed as the foundation of civilization, promoting love, productivity, and stability. Families efficiently pooled resources, raised children with strong moral and religious values, and ensured the continuation of family lineage. Marriage, as a sacred covenant, was integral to protecting against sexual immorality, fostering a stable environment for raising children, and sanctifying the union between a man and a woman. Procreation within the family was seen as a biological imperative, ensuring the survival of families, nations, and civilizations. The emphasis on marriage as a sacrament reinforced its role in maintaining the social fabric and promoting virtue within society.

The significance of marriage extended beyond personal relationships, impacting property ownership and inheritance in traditional Christendom. Marital stability was crucial for preserving family wealth and power, as property was closely tied to family lineage. The concentration of resources in the hands of the eldest male heir promoted the efficient management of family assets, ensuring that wealth and influence remained within the family. Divorce, while not encouraged, was sometimes permitted under strict conditions, with an emphasis on safeguarding family property and stability. These arrangements reflect the broader societal importance of family unity and resource preservation in a time when property was a cornerstone of status and influence.

The patriarchal influence on state authority, and its connection to the family, endures as a key chapter in the historical development of Western civilization. This legacy provides valuable insights into the foundations of family, property, and governance. Marriage and family life in traditional Christendom were influenced by a range of social, religious, and legal factors, emphasizing the role of consent in marriage. The Church played a central role in governing marriage, with the parish priest overseeing ceremonies and handling disputes. The Church's involvement underscored the sacred nature of marriage, grounded in faith, fidelity, and the raising of children within the Christian tradition.

The Church's teachings also addressed concerns about marriages between believers and non-believers, seeing such unions as threats to religious unity. Without a formal police force, families often took on law enforcement roles, with the father, or paterfamilias, settling disputes. Gender roles within the family were strictly defined, with the husband as the head of the household and the wife managing domestic affairs. Divorce laws evolved over time, influenced by early Church teachings, which gradually moved toward viewing marriage as indissoluble.

While separations were sometimes allowed, they typically revolved around issues of cruelty or adultery.

Traditional Christendom's approach to marriage and family life reflects the complex interplay between religious, social, and legal factors. The emphasis on consent, fidelity, and gender roles shaped societal expectations of marriage, ensuring that it remained a cornerstone of civilization. The role of children in traditional Christendom was also central to the family structure. Children were viewed as the means to carry forward family lineage, property, and values. Fathers bore the responsibility of providing education, discipline, and inheritance to ensure their children's future success. Legitimacy played a key role, with legitimate children granted certain rights and obligations, while illegitimate children were often excluded from inheritance and social standing.

The Reformation marked a significant shift in the relationship between family, Church, and state, with the separation of marriage from ecclesiastical jurisdiction and the growing influence of secular authorities. These changes reshaped the power dynamics within traditional Christendom, particularly regarding marriage and family life. The influence of celibacy within the Church, as well as the Protestant Reformation's impact on marriage, further highlights the evolving nature of family structures in Christian societies. Despite these changes, the legacy of traditional Christendom's emphasis on family, marriage, and children continues to resonate in contemporary debates about the role of family in society.

Bibliography

Catholic Church, & Libreria Editrice Vaticana. (1994). Catechism of the Catholic Church: revised in accordance with the official Latin text promulgated by Pope John Paul II. Libreria Editrice Vaticana,

Chrysostom, J., Roth, C. P., & Anderson, D. (1986). On marriage and family life. St. Vladimir's Seminary Press.

Desan, S., & University Of California Press. (2004). The family on trial in revolutionary France. University Of California Press, Berkley and Los Angeles, California.

Gies, Frances. Marriage and the Family in the Middle Ages (Medieval Life) (p. 3). HarperCollins. Kindle Edition.

Orsy, L. M. (1990). Marriage in canon law: texts and comments, reflections and questions. Liturgical Press.

Witte, J. (2012). From sacrament to contract: marriage, religion, and law in the Western tradition. Louisville (Kentucky); Westminster John Knox Press

Explore More from Sanctus Virtue Publishing
Championing Classical Virtue and Timeless Wisdom

Unveiling the Fall in the Garden of Eden: Classical and Modern Insights into the True Meaning of Original Sin: Upholding Baptismal Holiness and Overcoming

By Christopher Ross

ISBN: 979-8-9916647-5-2

This book offers a deep exploration of Original Sin's true meaning, tracing its roots to the Fall in the Garden of Eden and highlighting how Jesus' sacrifice and the sacraments empower Catholics to uphold baptismal holiness and overcome concupiscence, drawing on insights from classical and modern Christian teachings.

***

The French Revolution of 1789: Its War on the Classical Pillars of Western Society and the Rise of Secularism: Analysis of the Revolution's Attack on the Church, Monarchy, Tradition, and Patriarchy

By Christopher Ross

ISBN: 979-8991664707

Uncover the revolutionary upheavals that dismantled Western society's traditional foundations and led to the rise of secularism.

***

Catholic vs. Protestant Doctrine: Defending the Faith Against the Protestant Reformation's Heresies: A Catholic Apologetic Analysis of Sola Scriptura, Sola Fide, Purgatory, and Papal Infallibility

By Christopher Ross

ISBN: 979-8-9916647-1-4

An in-depth defense of Catholic doctrine, responding to the key Protestant reformations and providing insights into essential theological debates.

***

The Divine Balance: Authority, Governance, and Spiritual Supremacy in Traditional Christendom: Exploring the Interplay of Secular and Spiritual Powers from the Medieval Era to Modern America

By Christopher Ross

ISBN: 979-8-9916647-3-8

Examine the historical balance between secular authority and spiritual supremacy, and how this dynamic has evolved throughout Christendom.

www.ingramcontent.com/pod-product-compliance
Lightning Source LLC
Chambersburg PA
CBHW060848050426
42453CB00008B/890